101
AMAZING
OPTICAL
ILLUSIONS

Fantastic Visual Tricks

TERRY JENNINGS
Illustrated by Alex Pang

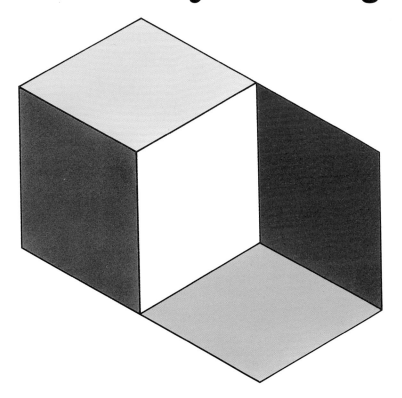

BARNES
&NOBLE
BOOKS
NEW YORK

This edition published by Barnes & Noble, Inc., by arrangement
with Sterling Publishing Company, Inc.

1997 Barnes & Noble Books

M 10 9 8 7 6 5 4 3 2 1

ISBN 0-7607-0624-7

Designer: Liz Black
Editor: Jenny Sharman
Computer-generated 3D artwork: Chris Winter,
Altered States Visuals Ltd.

Published by Sterling Publishing Company, Inc.
Originally published in Great Britain by Macdonald Young Books
© by Macdonald Young Books

Text © 1996 Terry Jennings
Illustrations © 1996 Alex Pang
Printed and bound in Hong Kong
All rights reserved

CONTENTS

INTRODUCTION

Here are 101 illusions for you to try out. Prepare to be intrigued! But first of all, what is an optical illusion? It is an image which deceives you into thinking it is something completely different from what it really is. It happens because of the way your eyes work, or the way your brain interprets what your eyes see, or even because of the nature of light itself. Sometimes even scientists do not know why an illusion works.

You can do a lot more with this book than simply read it, and for the most part the only equipment you need will be found around the home. Gather together some paper, poster board, pencils, a ruler, colors (in the form of paints, felt-tips or pencils), sticky tape and glue and have them ready, because once you start reading you will be itching to begin work on these practical projects. Each illusion comes with easy-to-follow, illustrated instructions, and tells you just what you need to do. Clear explanations throw light on why it works.

But the most important point about this book is that it is fun. You will discover how to put a bird in a cage, without touching it. You will learn how to break a spoon, and put it back together again without glue. You will be able to make ghostly shapes appear, see two pictures where there is only one, and make things change color – just using your eyes! There are lots of things you can do to make pictures move. You can get a whale to swim, a kangaroo to jump or a ballerina to dance. Moving pictures like these led to the invention of the movie and, later, television.

You will get even more out of this book when you share these illusions with friends and family. Remember to call an adult when you need to use scissors or sharp instruments. You have hours of pleasure ahead of you. Good luck, and remember, do not always believe what you see!

1

ON SIGHT

When your eyes tell you lies

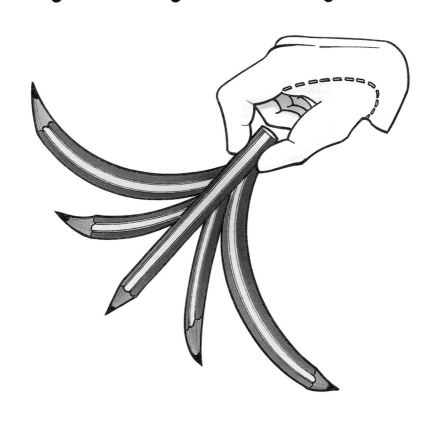

DOUBLE VISION

You have 3-D (three dimensional vision. Because of the distance between your eyes, each one sees things at a slightly different angle. Your brain brings the two images together and turns them into one all-embracing 3-D picture. This helps you to steer a bicycle without danger, shoot a basket, or thread a needle. If you put a patch over one eye, the world looks very flat, like a photograph. This is because you can see in only two dimensions instead of three.

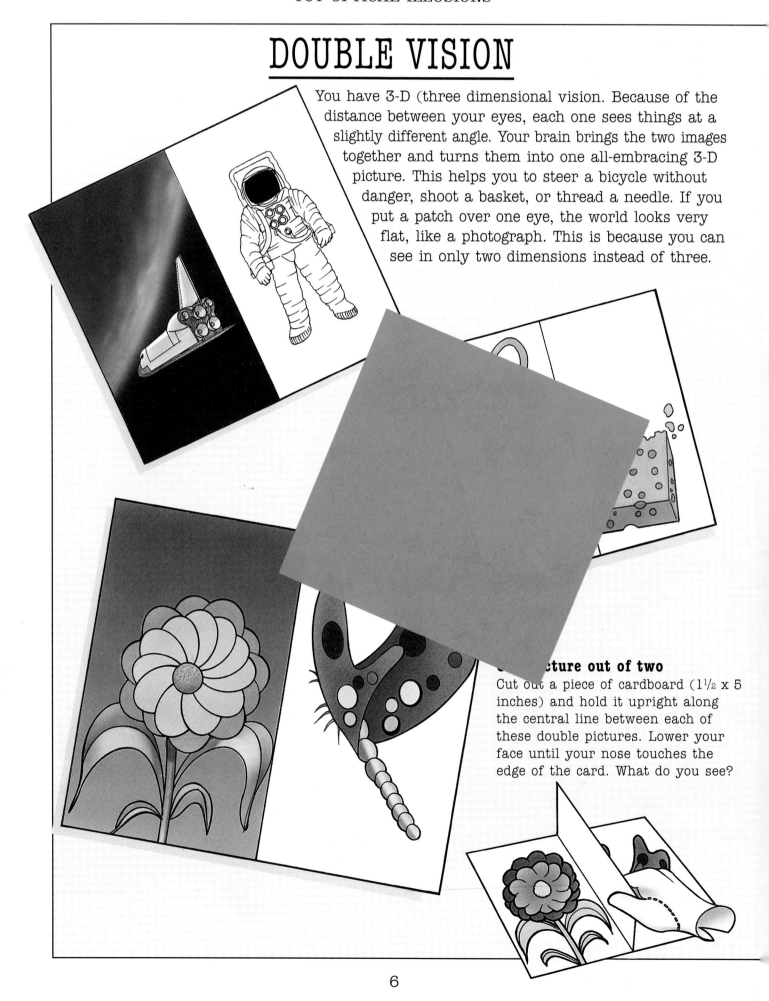

cture out of two

Cut out a piece of cardboard (1½ x 5 inches) and hold it upright along the central line between each of these double pictures. Lower your face until your nose touches the edge of the card. What do you see?

Put a hole in your hand

Here is a way to put a hole in your hand without pain or bloodshed. With your left eye, look through a small cardboard tube (a rolled sheet of paper fastened with tape will do). Bring your right hand, with the palm facing you, in front of your other eye. Keep both eyes open and look through the tube.

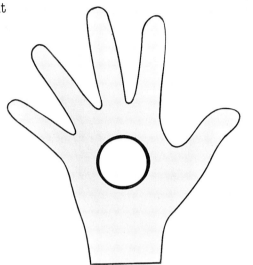

DOMINANT EYE

Chances are, if you are right-handed then you are right-eyed, too. Why not find out?

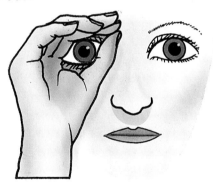

Make the fingers of one hand into a ring and look through it with both eyes at something across the room. Shut one eye. Can you still see the same thing, or has the ring jumped? Now try with the other eye shut. Whichever eye is open when you can see your chosen view is your dominant eye. This is the one you would probably use to look down a microscope or through a telescope or a magnifying glass.

The ghostly fingertip

To see double, hold the first finger of each hand about ½ an inch apart and about 1 foot in front of your eyes. Stare at a distant object such as a wall. You will see another image – a sausage-shaped fingertip – floating between your own fingertips. You are, in fact, seeing your fingers twice, once with each eye.

Stereograms

Find the hidden 3-D scene in the picture on the opposite page. Turn the book on its side. Make sure you are sitting in good light and stare at something on the other side of the room for 20 seconds. Then, keeping the same focus, quickly raise the book so your nose touches the center of the picture. Keeping the book upright, move it slowly away from your face. At some point, the 3-D image will come into focus. This needs practice, so stick with it (the picture on this page is an advance view).

To create a stereogram, a computer first produces a black and white representation of a 3-D scene, called a greyscale (above). The greyscale indicates depth by showing the nearest areas as white and the furthest areas as black, with shades of gray in between. Next comes the noisefield, processed by the computer as thousands of tiny dots. The computer repeats the noisefield again and again, "covering" the greyscale. Where the greyscale is lighter, the computer rearranges the dots in the noisefield so that they are closer together. Where the greyscale is darker, the dots are further apart. This gives the stereogram pattern a distorted appearance (see left).

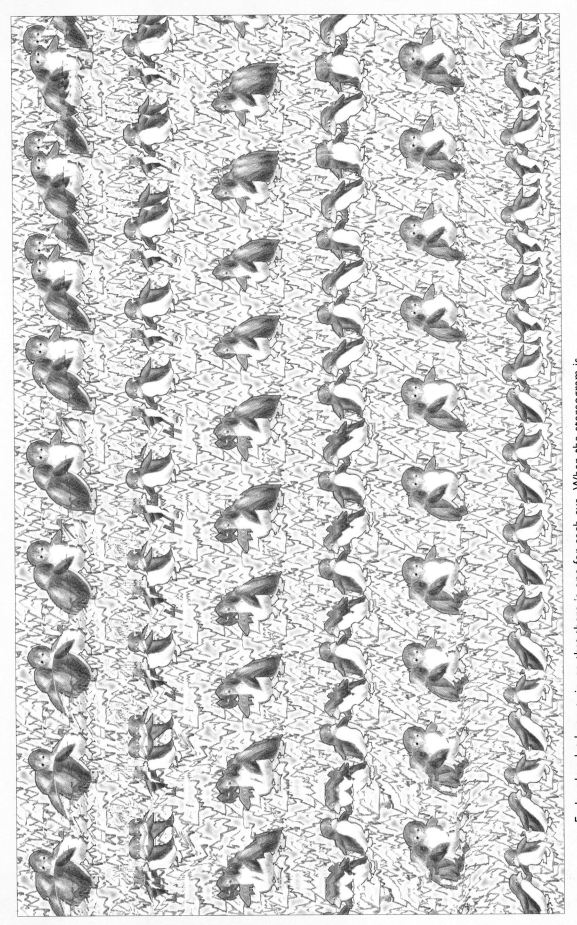

Each color dot has a twin, so that there is one for each eye. When the stereogram is viewed correctly, the left eye's view and the right eye's view overlap to produce a 3-D image in the brain.

OP ART

One reason for the whirling sensation you get from staring at these vivid pictures is that they disturb your eyes and force them to increase the number of small movements they usually make. Your eyes make these slight movements all day. They are important in helping you to see things clearly, and in giving the eye muscles some good exercise. Your eyes do get time off at night. They relax with the rest of you when you sleep, and roll back in your head!

Wheels within wheels

To get the full effect from each of these illusions, move the book from side to side and then stop and stare for a few moments. Even though you have stopped moving, they have not. You may even see some bicycle spokes.

Flashing figure

Stare at this for a few moments.
The flashing sensation will drive
your brain to the wrong
conclusions.

Imaginary dots

Stare at the blank
spaces between the
columns and you will
see some moving dots.

Starburst

Stare at the center and watch this whirl.
Can you see any colors?

Magic carpet
This pattern of wavy lines looks as if it might
flutter in the wind like a flag, or rise and float
away like a magic carpet.

HOW TO MAKE A QUIVERING TOP

These twirling tops will make your head spin.

1 Photocopy one of the disks on the next page and paste it onto some cardboard. Or trace the design onto cardboard and color it in. Cut neatly around the disk and pierce a small hole in the center.

2 Bend one end of a paper clip so that it sticks out at a right angle to the rest of the clip. Hold the clip so that the straightened wire stands up and slip the disk onto it, resting it lightly on your thumb and first finger.

3 Spin the disk slightly. Then stop it and stare. Spin the disk the other way and do the same again. See whether it makes any difference.

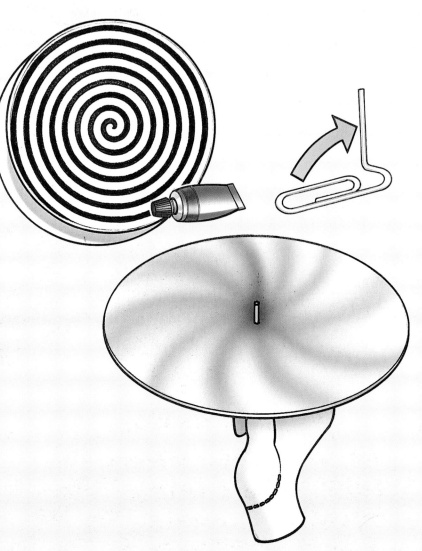

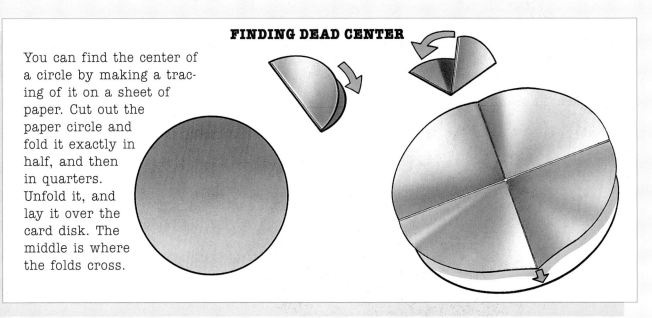

FINDING DEAD CENTER

You can find the center of a circle by making a tracing of it on a sheet of paper. Cut out the paper circle and fold it exactly in half, and then in quarters. Unfold it, and lay it over the card disk. The middle is where the folds cross.

When you spin your disks, which one seems to shrink and expand? Which one seems to move in both directions at once?

BENDING LIGHT

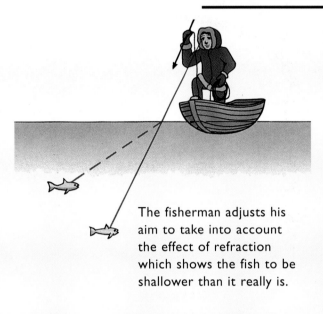

The fisherman adjusts his aim to take into account the effect of refraction which shows the fish to be shallower than it really is.

We can only see things because light, which always travels in straight lines, bounces off them and into our eyes. But something curious happens when light rays get bent. For one thing, have you ever noticed that your legs and feet look short and chunky when you are in a swimming pool and that the water looks shallower than it really is? If you could measure it, you would find that the real depth of the water is about one-and-a-third times as deep as it looks. This happens because the light beams are changing direction just a little every time they move backwards or forwards between air, water or glass. This is known as refraction.

Make a coin appear
Try this trick with a friend. Stand a cup on a table and put a coin into it. Slowly move the cup away from you until you can no longer see the coin. Stay where you are and ask your friend to pour some water into the cup. The coin will suddenly reappear.

Break a spoon
Stand a teaspoon in a glass half filled with water and hold the glass so that it is level with your eyes. This gives you the best view of the "break" in the spoon. You will see the same effect if you hold a pencil partly behind a thick glass bowl.

MAKE A STAMP DISAPPEAR

Amaze your friends by making
a stamp disappear with the
help of a "magic" card.

1 Lay a postage stamp on the
table and place a glass of
water on top of it.

2 Cover the top of the glass with a
piece of stiff paper (a postcard
will do). You will not be able
to see the stamp from any
direction. This is because
the light rays are refracted
upwards when they pass
from the stamp, through
the glass of water into the
air. The card screens off all
the refracted rays and keeps
you from seeing the stamp.

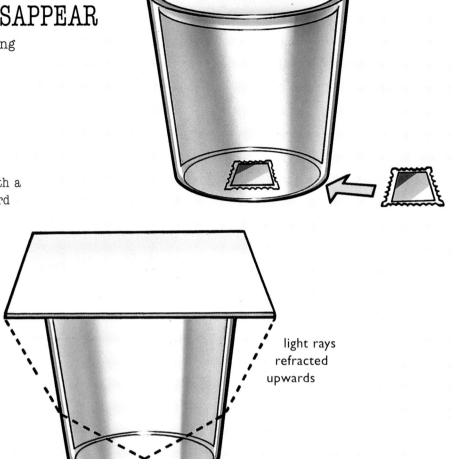

light rays
refracted
upwards

FLOATING IN THE AIR

Sometimes thirsty travelers in the desert
think they see a shimmering pool of water.
This is not their imagination, but a mirage.
On hot, clear days with no wind, the air
closest to the ground is hotter than the air
above it and the light passing through the
boundary between the warmer and colder
air is bent. You see things that are not
really there like a pool of water that is
actually an image of the sky. In the summer,
you may see a mirage of pools of water
appear on a hot road ahead of you. Mirages
also appear near the North and South Poles,
so that distant objects, such as ships, appear
much nearer and can seem to be floating in
the sky, as in this picture.

ON REFLECTION

Mirrors do strange things to images. For example, you can never see yourself in a mirror as you really are. Stand in front of one and try it for yourself. When you stand opposite a friend and both raise your right hands, these hands are on opposite sides. But when you stand in front of a mirror and raise your right hand, your image appears to raise its left hand. Why? Because light rays bounce back off the mirror towards you, so you see a reversed image. We take mirrors and the illusions they show us pretty much for granted. Try these tricks and you can rediscover some mirror magic.

MAKE A KALEIDOSCOPE

1 Have ready some mirrored cardboard, a few small beads and sequins, sticky tape, scissors, colorless cellophane or white tissue paper, a ruler and some thin white paper.

2 Make a tracing of the rectangle (right) and use it to draw and cut out three rectangles from the mirrored cardboard.

3 Trace the triangle (below) and, using it as a guide, cut out one triangle from the cellophane or tissue paper and two from the thin white paper.

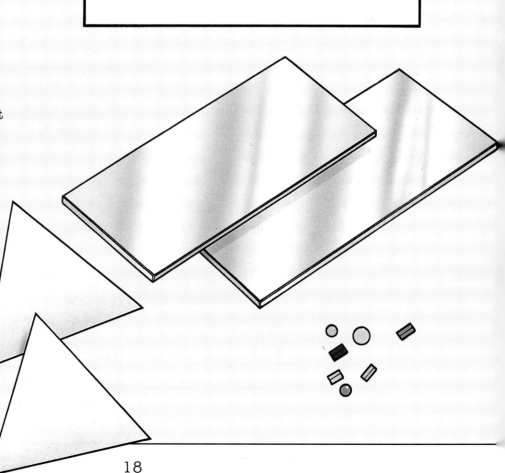

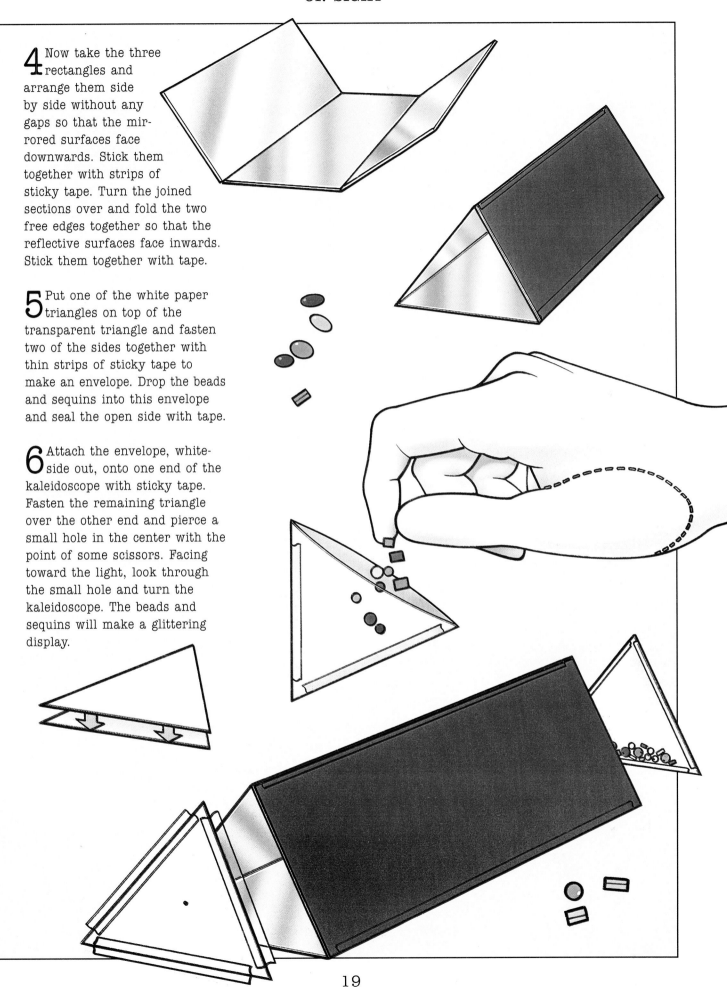

4 Now take the three rectangles and arrange them side by side without any gaps so that the mirrored surfaces face downwards. Stick them together with strips of sticky tape. Turn the joined sections over and fold the two free edges together so that the reflective surfaces face inwards. Stick them together with tape.

5 Put one of the white paper triangles on top of the transparent triangle and fasten two of the sides together with thin strips of sticky tape to make an envelope. Drop the beads and sequins into this envelope and seal the open side with tape.

6 Attach the envelope, white-side out, onto one end of the kaleidoscope with sticky tape. Fasten the remaining triangle over the other end and pierce a small hole in the center with the point of some scissors. Facing toward the light, look through the small hole and turn the kaleidoscope. The beads and sequins will make a glittering display.

Funny faces

Put a pocket mirror, on its edge, down the center of this face, so that it reflects one side of it. Study the face and then flip the mirror over to reflect the other side. What difference does it make? You can try this with a full-face photograph of yourself, someone in your family or a friend. See what you would look like if your face was quite symmetrical. But first, search for the clowns hidden in the image below by moving the mirror, still on its edge, from place to place, studying the reflections you create.

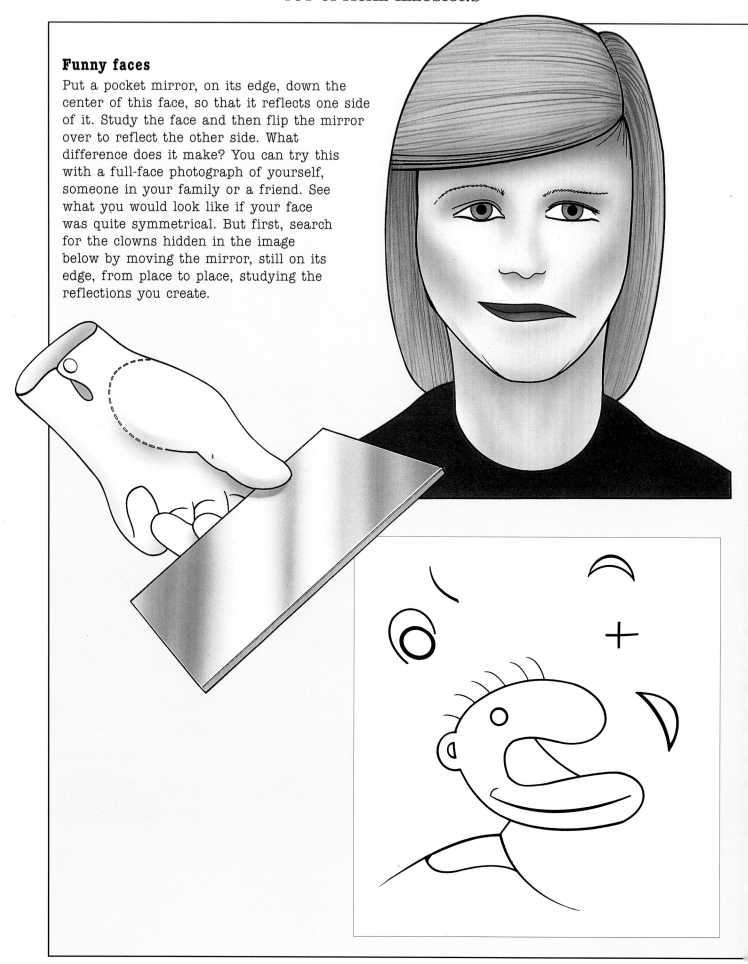

Mirror writing

Hold this book up to a mirror and look at these words. What is so special about them? Still looking at the reflection, turn the book upside down. Can you make some words that will act in the same way?

Back to front

Write the numbers one to ten in a random pattern all over the middle of a sheet of paper. Hold a mirror in one hand at the end of the piece of paper and, only looking at the reflection, try to draw a line through all the numbers in the right order. Make the line as straight as possible. This is not as easy as you might think.

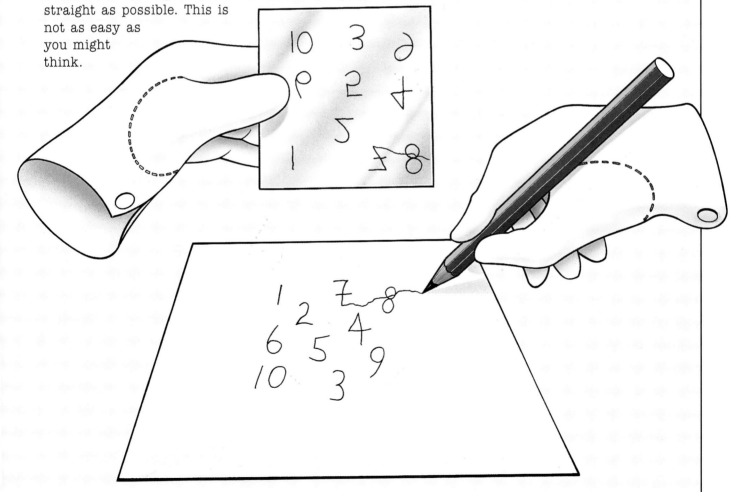

INNER EYE

As you have now discovered, the way our eyes are designed and built has a great deal to do with why we see optical illusions. Here are some more ways in which our eyes play their own tricks on us.

Blanking out

Close your right eye. Hold this page about 10 inches away from you and stare hard at the face. Move the book slowly from side to side, keeping your eye fixed. You will see the bull's-eye disappear when its image hits the spot where the optic nerve leaves the back of the eye. This is the only area of the retina not sensitive to light. The brain compensates for this, so that in everyday life we may not notice that we have this blind spot.

A curved ball

Take a good look at these checked circles. The one on the left is made up of even-sized squares while those in the one on the right are uneven. But if you bring the left-hand circle about an inch away from one eye, it will bulge out toward you. When you do the same to the right-hand circle, the squares seem to become regular. The reason? The retina at the back of the eye is curved, something you are unlikely to have noticed because you rarely use the whole of the retina at one time.

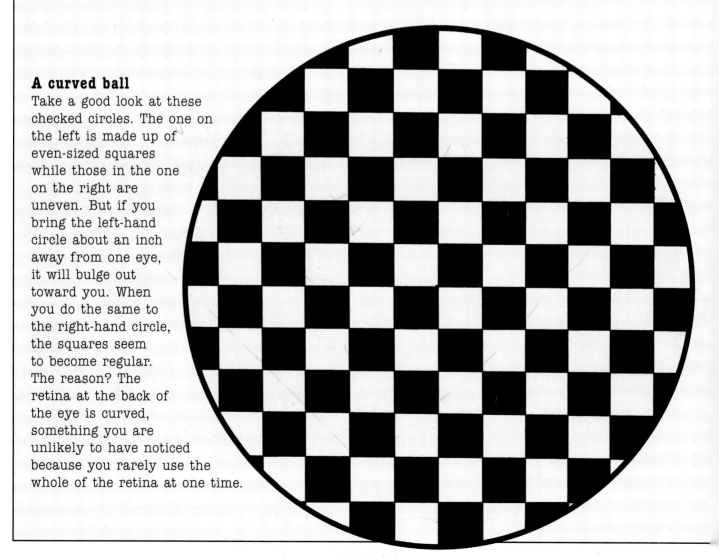

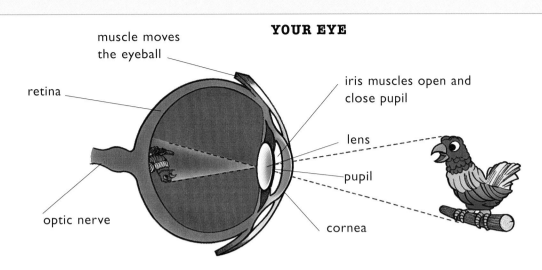

YOUR EYE

- muscle moves the eyeball
- retina
- optic nerve
- iris muscles open and close pupil
- lens
- pupil
- cornea

Your eye is a liquid-filled ball with a transparent window at the front (the cornea). This bends rays of light through the pupil and then through the lens which focuses them onto a sensitive screen (the retina) at the back of the eye. Our eyes actually see things upside down and backwards because the rays of light go straight to the retina. The optic nerve sends messages about the image from the retina to the brain, which then sorts these out so that you see things the right way up.

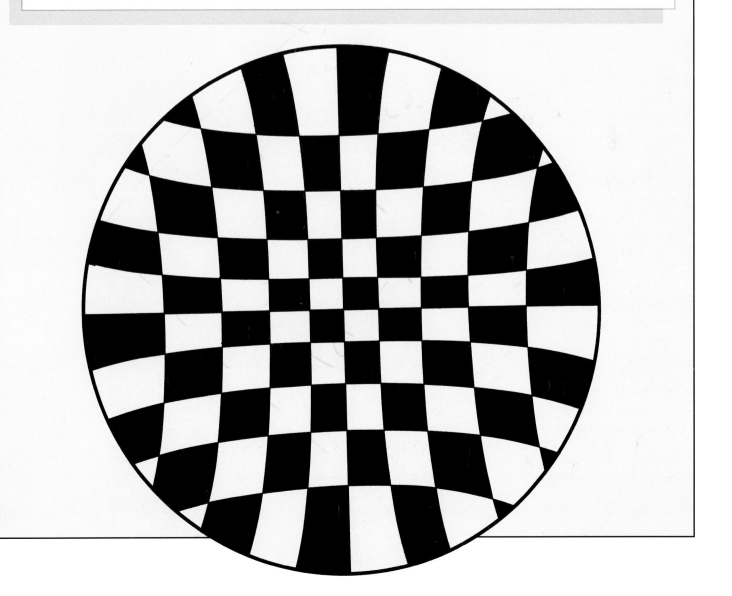

IN FULL COLOR

Light comes mainly from the sun, but it is not what it seems. Although it is called white light, it is made up of a rainbow of different shades. And this means that you can conjure with color.

MAKE A FEATHERY SPECTRUM

The first person to split light was Sir Isaac Newton, over four hundred years ago. He used a prism (a triangular piece of glass). You can split light and see its rainbow colors just with the aid of a feather. But never do this without an adult present.

1 Set a candle in a candlestick safely on a table and light it. Darken the room.

2 Stand about a foot away from the candle, close one eye and hold a large, clean feather near your other eye. Look through it at the candle flame. When the light passes through the narrow slits of the feather, it splits up. You will see several little patches of light, each with a fringe of rainbow colors—images of the flame.

3 Still looking through the feather, carefully move back from the candle. You will see even more images of the candle flame. What happens if you slowly rotate the feather? Do the images of the flame also turn?

4 When you have finished, blow out the candle!

MAKE A SPINNER

You can also see how the process works in reverse. Join up the separate colors of the rainbow by making a spinning top.

1 Use a cup to draw a circle on a piece of white cardboard and divide the disk into seven equal areas. If you prefer, you can make a tracing of the disk on this page.

2 Color each segment in a different color of the spectrum. It does not matter which order you put them in.

3 Find the center of the disk and push a pencil stub through it to make a spinner. Spin the disk on a smooth surface. While the disk is spinning quickly, your eyes will not be able to make out the separate colors. If you could use absolutely pure colors, the disk would look white, but with ordinary paints and felt-tips the colors will tend to merge into a grayish-white.

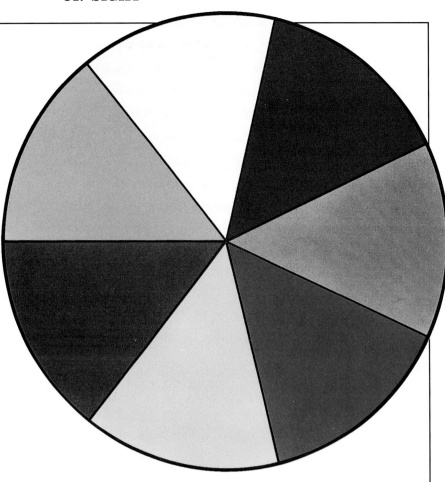

Try making spinners with the colors in a different order or try two colors, one on each half. Does it make any difference to the effect? You can also make this into a twirler (see page 72).

SEEING COLORS

Light consists of seven colors in more than 100 shades. This is known as the visible spectrum. Each one has its own wavelength, and because our eyes are able to distinguish one of these from another, we have color vision. Exactly which color we see depends on the wavelength of light that the object we are looking at reflects. Anything we look at will reflect some of the colors of white light and absorb, or soak up, others. A red car reflects red light and absorbs most of the other colors in white light. A black car absorbs all the colors, and a white one reflects them all.

AFTEREFFECTS

You are about to encounter some afterimages. You will know what this means if you have ever been on the receiving end of a camera flash bulb, and remember the black "shadow" that appears afterward in front of your eyes. It usually takes just a moment or two to recover normal vision. Before you begin looking at these pictures, sit under a bright light. Stare hard at one of these images for 30 seconds to a minute without blinking too much. Try not to move your eyes. When the time is up, look quickly at the white square close by on the page, and watch the magic work. (If nothing happens the first time, try again, this time eyeing the picture for a little longer). Staring at the image overstimulates the parts of the retina you have been using and this causes you to see an afterimage. Try the same trick with the images you will find on the next two pages.

Clowning about
Stare at the clown's nose.

Identify the flag

This flag may look strange as it is, but you can make it turn into the red, white and blue Union Jack. Do the same with the one below and it will begin to resemble the flag of the U.S.A.

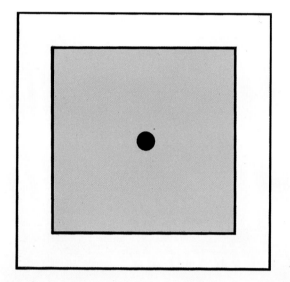

Seeing red
What color is the border around this square? What about the inside of the square, and the dot? Why not try drawing other shapes and other combinations of colors.

Black to white
Can you make this bulb light up?

Songbird
Stare at the red bird for about 30 seconds. Then stare at the cage. It may help if you blink. Gradually a green bird will emerge inside the cage.

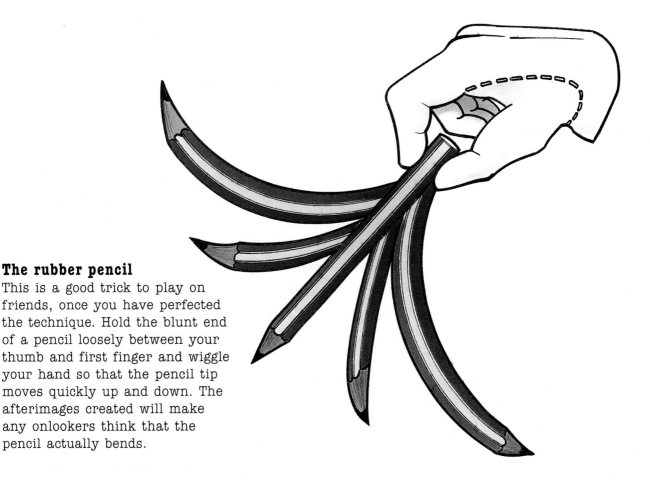

The rubber pencil
This is a good trick to play on friends, once you have perfected the technique. Hold the blunt end of a pencil loosely between your thumb and first finger and wiggle your hand so that the pencil tip moves quickly up and down. The afterimages created will make any onlookers think that the pencil actually bends.

MAKE A TRANSFORMER

Many people see colors when these disks spin. No one knows for certain why this happens. It may be because the retina gets tired and sees colors as an afterimage, or it could be that the spinning disk splits up white light into the various colors of the spectrum (see page 24).

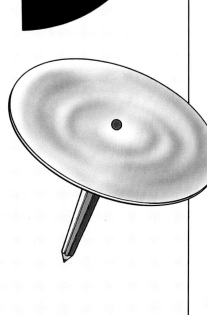

1 If you can, photocopy these discs and stick them onto pieces of cardboard with some glue or paste. Or trace the designs and transfer them onto the piece of cardboard. Go over the lines with a black felt tip pen and fill them in where necessary.

2 Cut neatly around each disk. Push a pin or thumbtack through the center of one disk and fasten it loosely to the eraser at the end of a pencil. Spin the disk to see the colors. Then try it with the other disk.

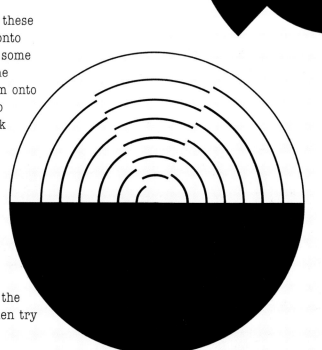

SEEING AN AFTERIMAGE

Scientists do not yet know all they need to about the cells (cones) in the retina which "see" color, but it seems that some are more sensitive to red, some to green, some to blue, and probably some to yellow.

An afterimage follows when the cones in the retina become tired after staring hard at something for a short time. When you look at something else right away, only the rested cones will respond.

An afterimage appears in the color that is opposite (complementary) to the color of the original. White stimulates all the cones, and so you will always see the afterimage in black.

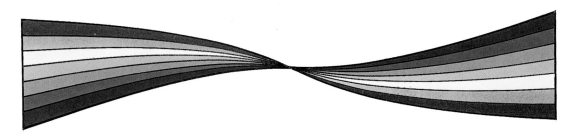

2
ON PERCEPTION
Why your brain takes the strain

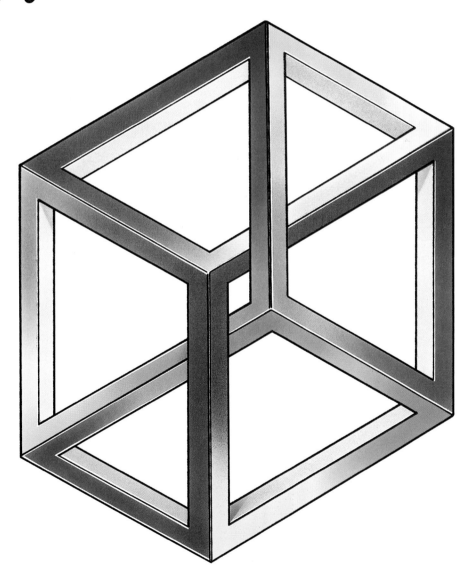

GHOSTS BEFORE YOUR EYES

The brain's job is to make sense of what the eyes are seeing. That is what we mean by "perception." Most of the time the brain does just fine, but occasionally it jumps to the wrong conclusions when it follows clues that are misleading. The brain tries to make sense of the images below by filling in what it perceives are gaps. It decides there is an invisible shape at the front which partly hides the visible one behind it.

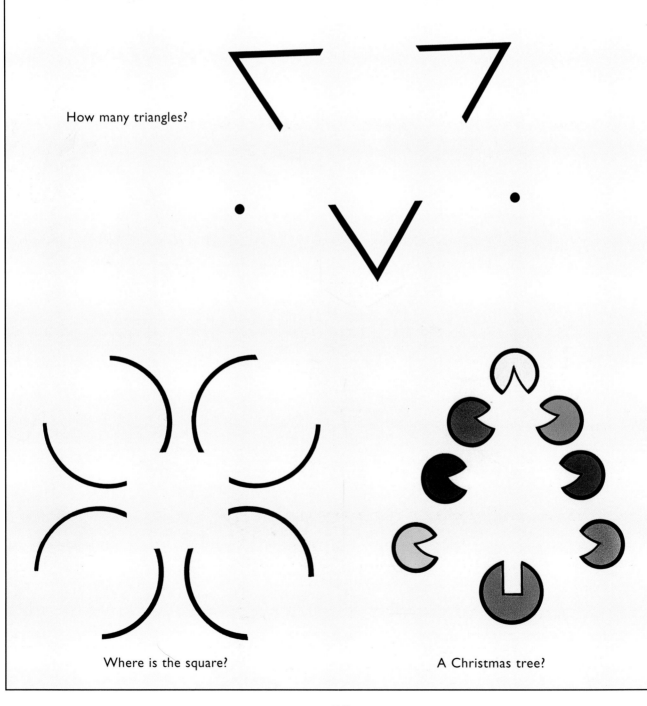

How many triangles?

Where is the square?

A Christmas tree?

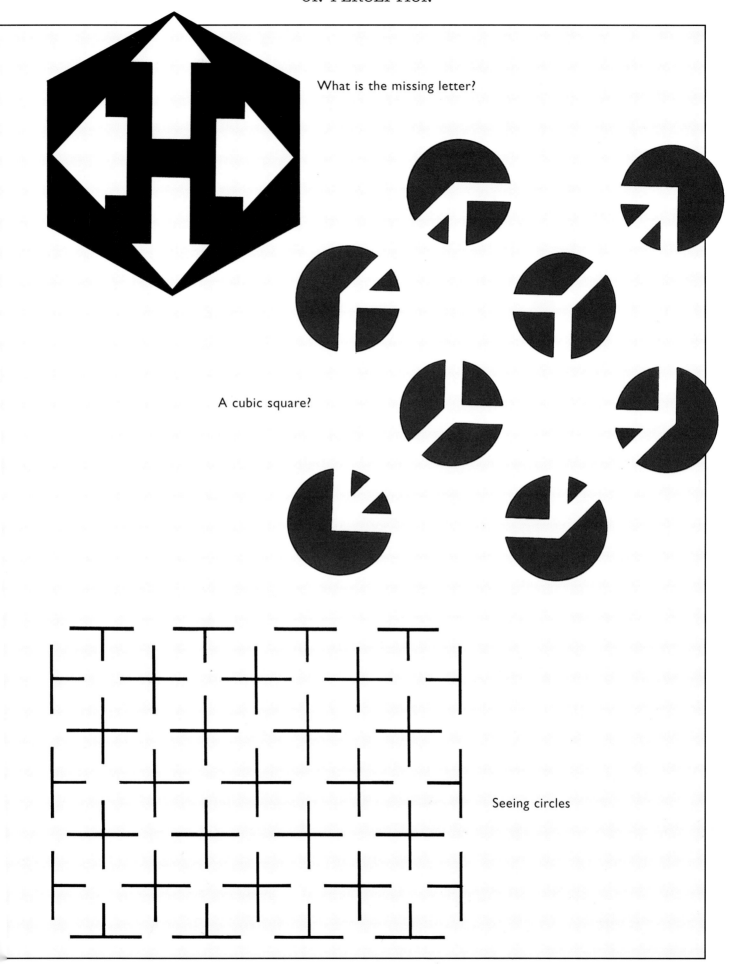

What is the missing letter?

A cubic square?

Seeing circles

SHAPE SHIFTERS

The background of a picture can be just as important as what is in front. Look at the two pictures below. The figure on the far right in each picture is exactly the same, but you see it as entirely different, because of its context. All of the lines you see on the next four pages are straight, and all the shapes are regular, but they do not look it. They appear misshapen because of what is going on around them. People have tried for hundreds of years to explain these illusions but no one really understands why most of us see the same distortions.

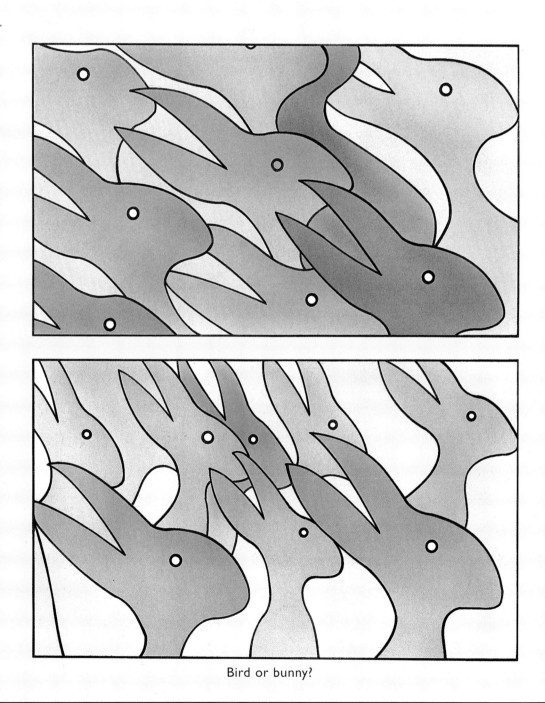

Bird or bunny?

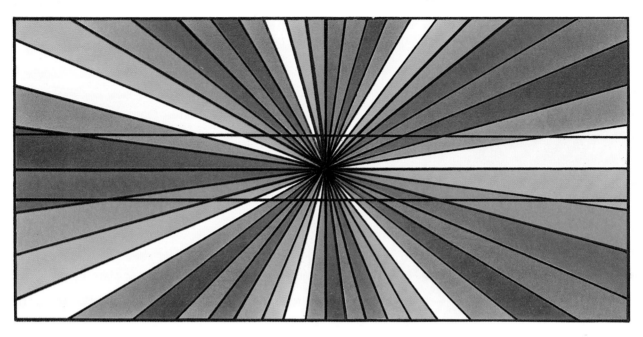

Not-so-parallel lines

TRUE OR FALSE

You may find it helpful and amusing to draw the main parts of some of these illusions on heavy paper. You can then see clearly how your eyes deceive you. Cut a sheet of clear plastic and the paper to the same size. On the paper, measure and copy, or trace, the parts of each illusion that are the same. Cover the paper with the overlay and tape them together at the top. Draw the remaining parts of the illusion on the overlay.

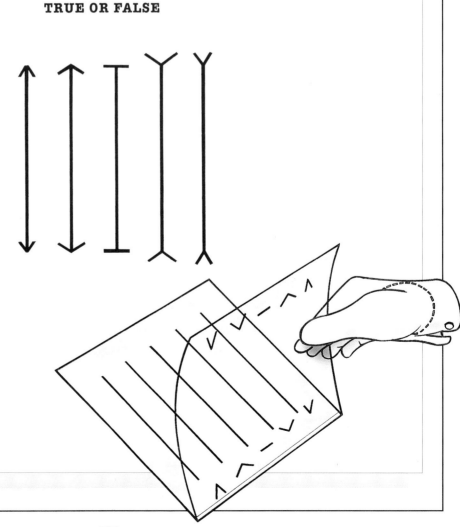

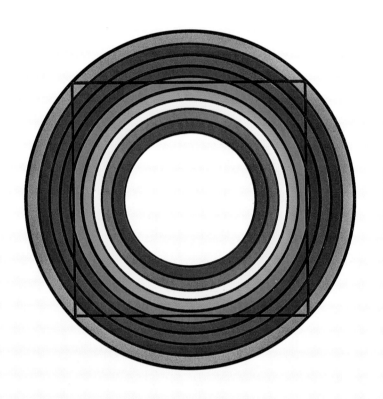

Perfect square?
Does this square really bend toward the middle?

Soft circle and tilted square?
How do these radiating lines affect the circle and square?

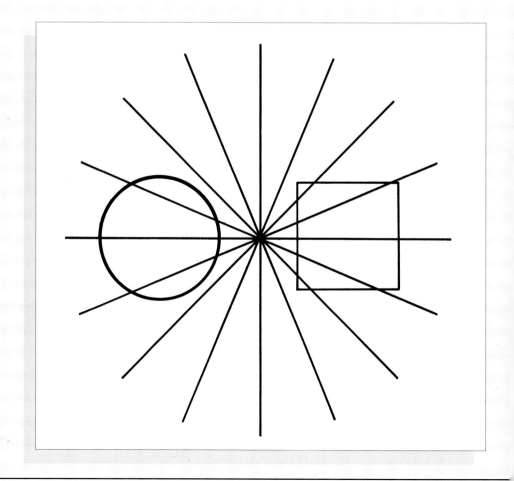

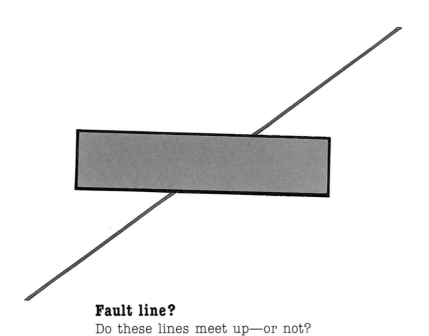

Fault line?
Do these lines meet up—or not?

On the slant?
These long lines seem quite random.
Can you tell whether they are parallel?

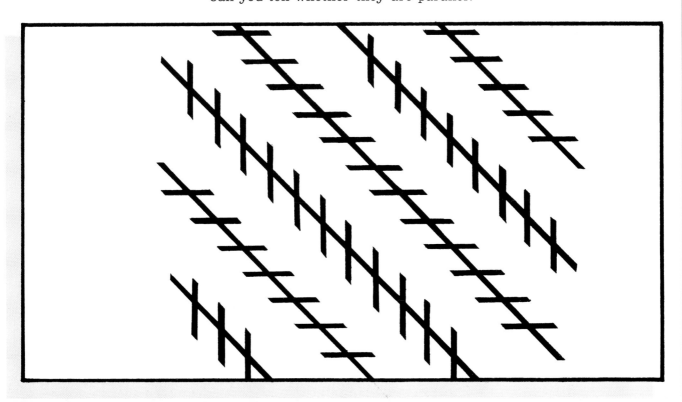

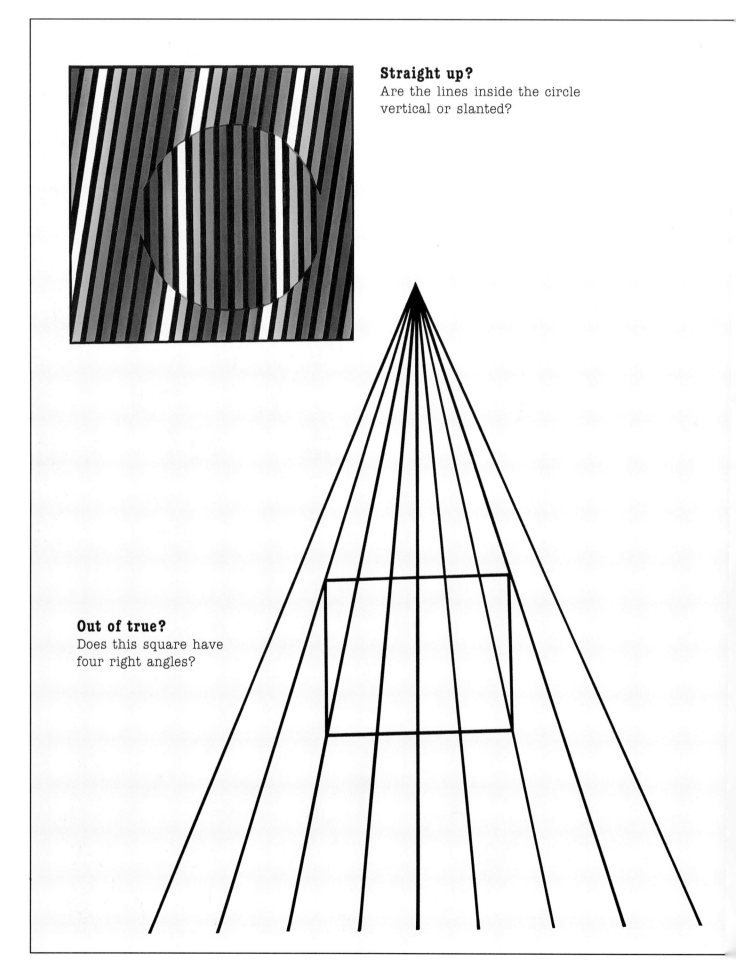

Straight up?
Are the lines inside the circle
vertical or slanted?

Out of true?
Does this square have
four right angles?

The tiled wall

Are the tiles square or wedge-shaped? The distortion is even greater if you look at it out of the corner of your eye. Check and you will find that all the tiles have parallel sides and are laid parallel to each other.

Same difference

How we see colors can depend on which other colors are near them. Look at the two gray ovals at the right. Which gray is the lighter shade?

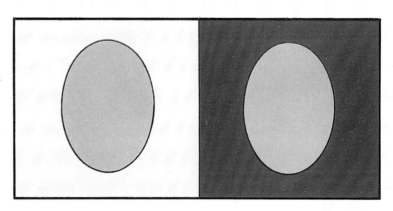

JUDGING THE SIZE

It is not always easy to judge shape, but it can be even harder to judge size or length, as you are about to see. There have been many suggestions as to how the following illusions produce their effects, and you will find some of the possible explanations below, but no one knows for certain what the answers are.

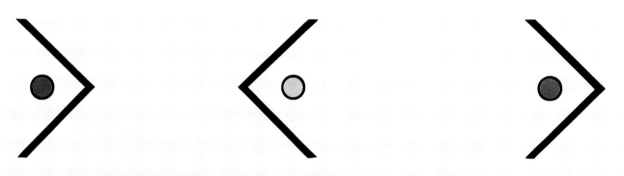

Near or far?
Are these three dots the same distance apart?

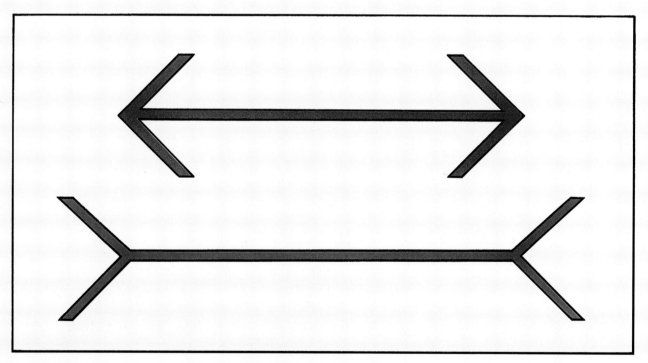

The Muller-Lyer illusion

This well-known illusion is named after the German scientist who discovered it in 1889. The line with arrows pointing toward each other looks much longer than the line with the arrows pointing away from each other. And yet, if you measure, you will find that they are both the same length.

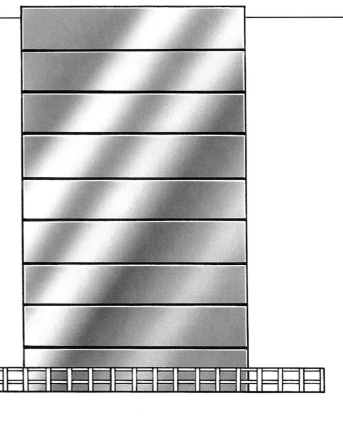

High or wide?

Which is the greater, the height of the building or the length of the fence at its base?

UNDER THE INFLUENCE

When you try to compare the lines and shapes here, you may well be influenced without even realizing it. For example, angles that are less than 90 degrees can make a line look shorter, while angles of more than 90 degrees can make it look longer – as the Muller-Lyer illusion shows. Also, it takes more effort to look up and down than from side to side, and so we tend to think that lines going from the top to the bottom of the page are longer than the same lines going across the page. Light-colored areas generally look larger than dark ones, which, in turn, look heavier than light ones. However, there are exceptions to these rules, as the first illusion at the top of the opposite page shows. In this box, look at the image on the far left; are the horizontal lines the same length? In the right-hand image, are the two lines the same or different?

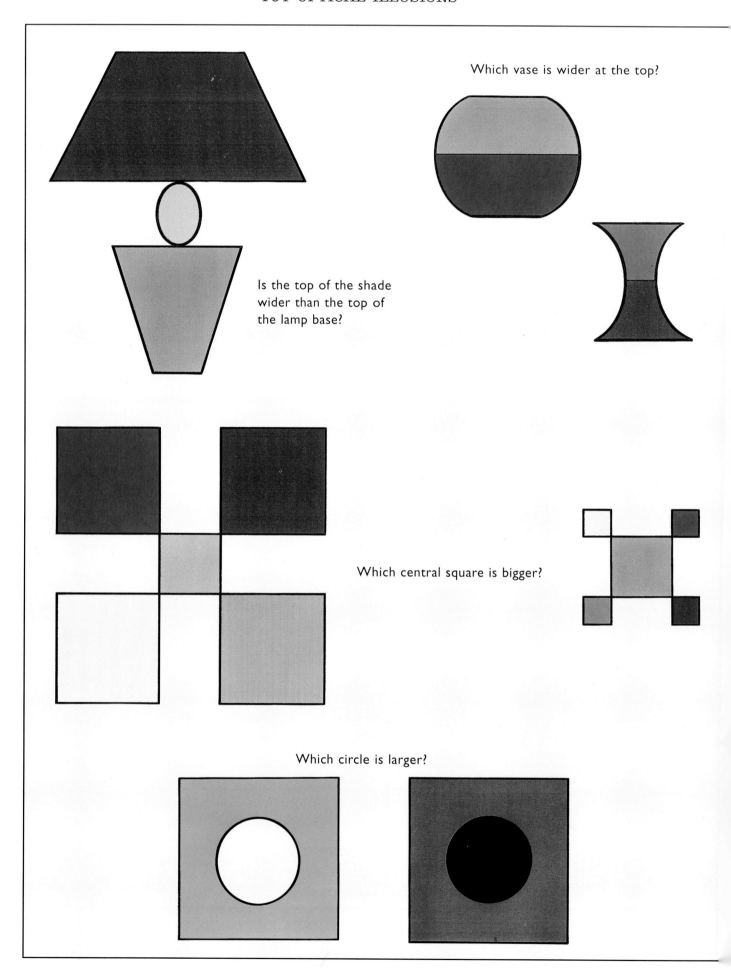

Which vase is wider at the top?

Is the top of the shade wider than the top of the lamp base?

Which central square is bigger?

Which circle is larger?

MAKE A MAGIC CURVE

Prove to yourself that this is an illusion by making these two shapes for yourself! You will find that whichever curve is placed above the other, the lower one always looks larger. This is because the upper edge of the lower shape is longer than the lower edge of the upper shape. Try this on a friend.

1 Trace one of the outlines (right) and use it to cut out two curves from a piece of heavy white paper. Leave one white and color the other one in.

2 Place the two curves on a table, so that they are parallel to each other. Which curve looks bigger?

INTO PERSPECTIVE

When you watch someone walking down the road, the farther away they are, the smaller they seem to be. Artists use this rule of perspective to give a flat surface depth. You could say that their pictures are optical illusions. We apply the same rule without even thinking about it – and that is how we get caught out!

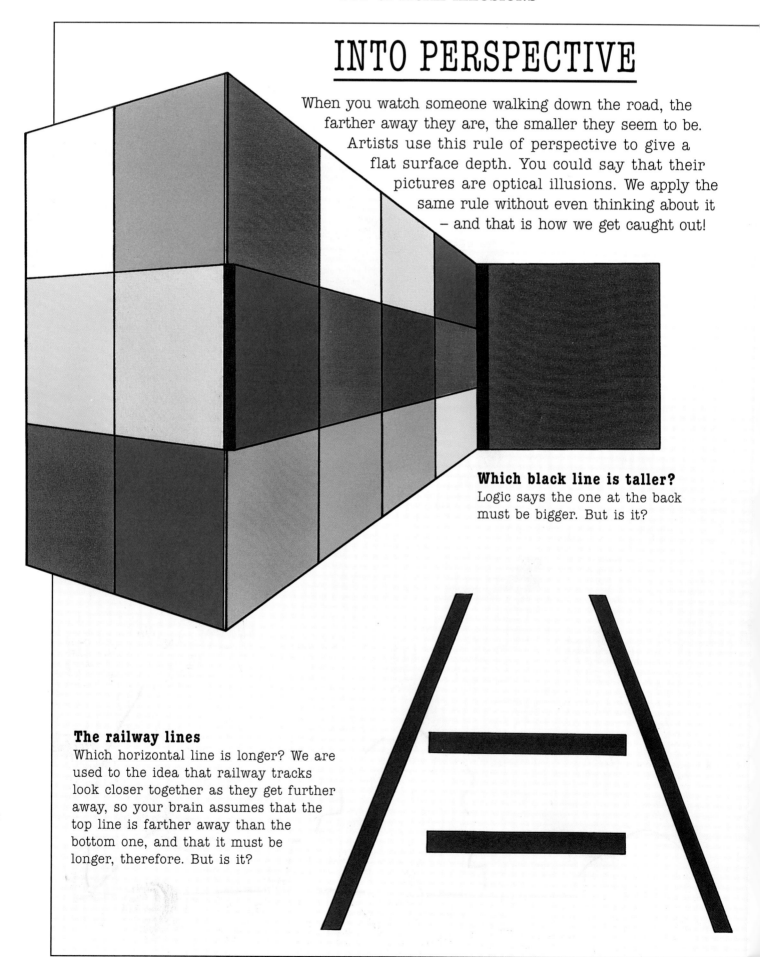

Which black line is taller?
Logic says the one at the back must be bigger. But is it?

The railway lines
Which horizontal line is longer? We are used to the idea that railway tracks look closer together as they get further away, so your brain assumes that the top line is farther away than the bottom one, and that it must be longer, therefore. But is it?

GIVING DEPTH

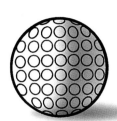

These two balls look the same size when you see them straight on. The truth emerges only when you see them from above. Without the help of perspective, the picture lacks depth and you have no clues as to the true relationship between things in the picture. Which is the football and which the golf ball?

Viewed from above

Tunnel vision
Who is the tallest pedestrian?

The tiled room
The wall becomes a floor near the middle of the image. The change from trapezoids in the lower part of the figure to squares in the upper part does the trick.

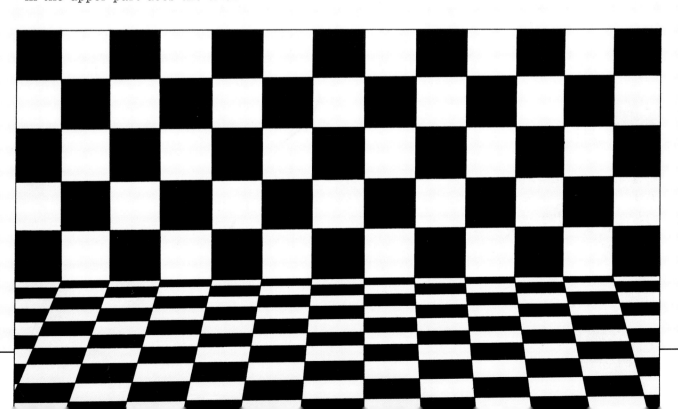

The floating balls

This drawing comes to life if you stare at it for a few seconds. The light-colored balls seem to hover above the page. Using shadow, the artist makes this much more realistic by giving the picture depth.

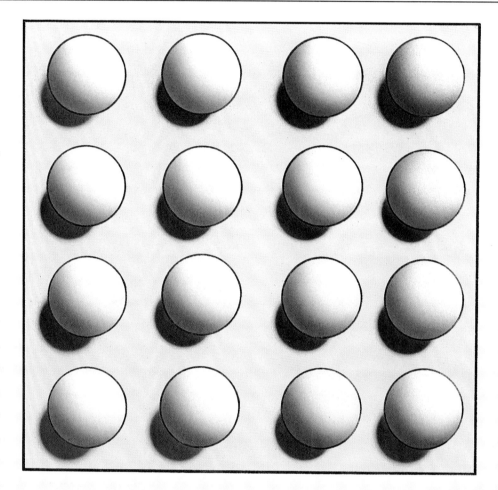

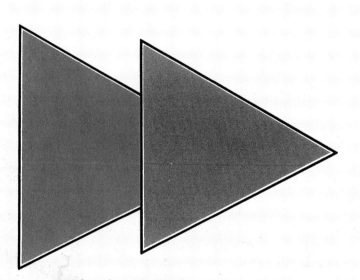

Which image is on top?

Most people see this as one triangle on top of another. Few see it as two shapes that are side by side.

Standing sticks

Turn the book slightly, so that the corner is in front of you, and look at the image in the direction of the arrow. Tip it slightly away from you. Close one eye and look at the lines. They should seem to stand straight up off the page.

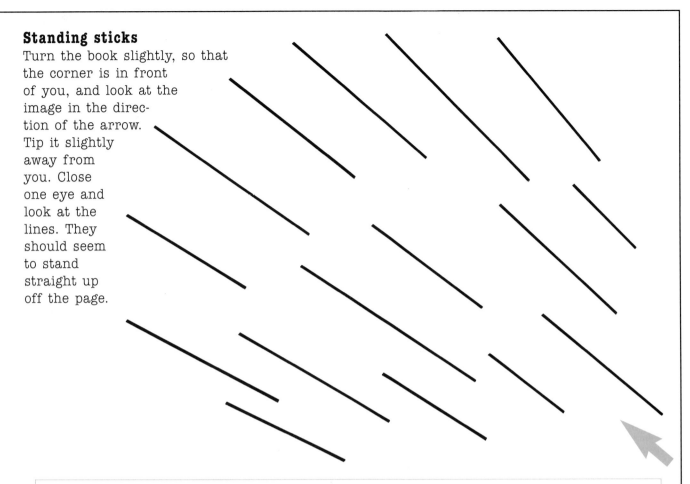

AN EXAGGERATED SIGN

Distortion can be very useful. The bicycle (right) has been pulled completely out of shape, but if you see it while traveling on the road at full speed, it will look quite normal, and might stop you in your tracks. This is called an anamorphic image, and pictures using the same trick were painted as long ago as the fifteenth century, when they were used to mystify and amaze an audience.

OUT OF THIS WORLD

Four in one
Imagine walking up this staircase from the bottom left-hand side. How many steps are there? Now start from the bottom right. How many are there now?

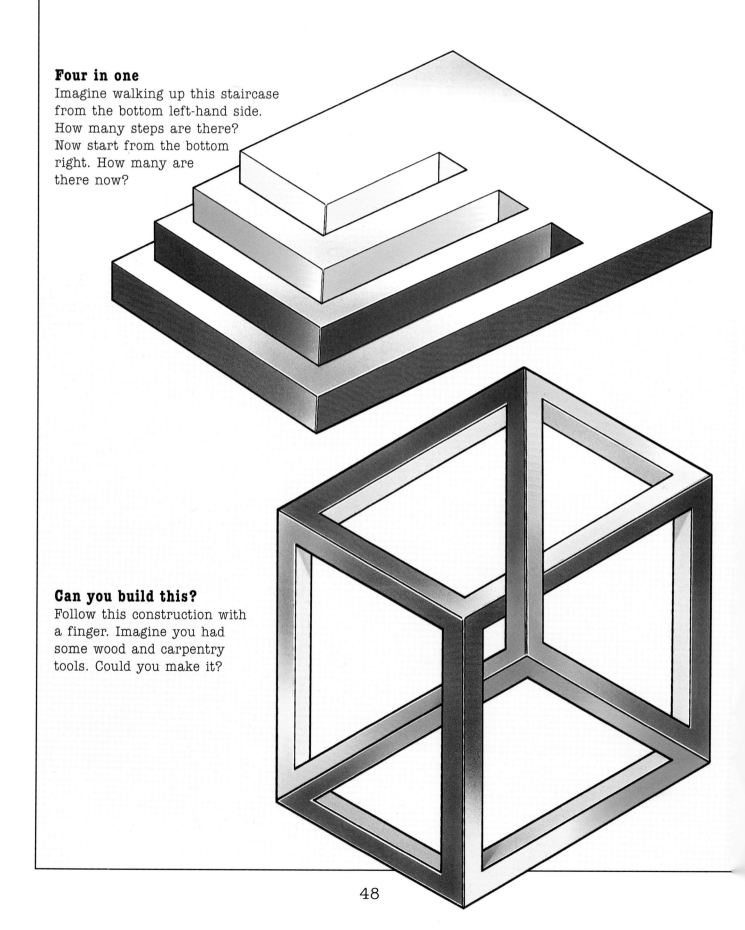

Can you build this?
Follow this construction with a finger. Imagine you had some wood and carpentry tools. Could you make it?

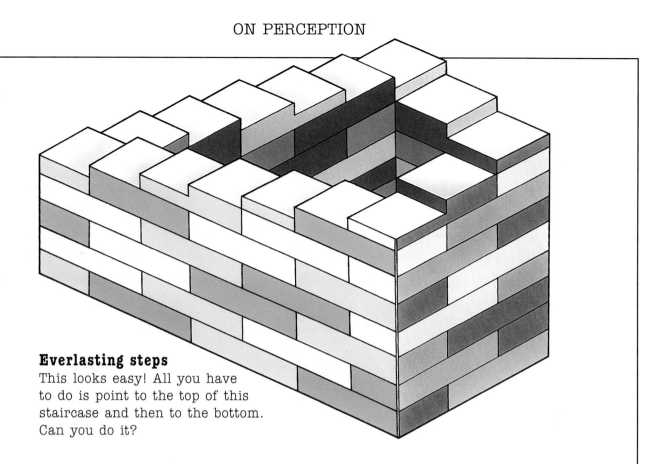

Everlasting steps

This looks easy! All you have
to do is point to the top of this
staircase and then to the bottom.
Can you do it?

THE IMPROBABLE ELEPHANT

Look at the legs of this elephant.
Can you count them? Where
does each leg join the
animal's body?

TWO IN ONE

If you look at each of these pictures carefully, you will see two different figures. You may not be able to see both figures at first. Once you have, you may find that they jump in and out of view from time to time, but you will not be able to see both of them at once. Try these pictures on your friends. Which figure do they see first?

A man or a rat

A mosque or two heads

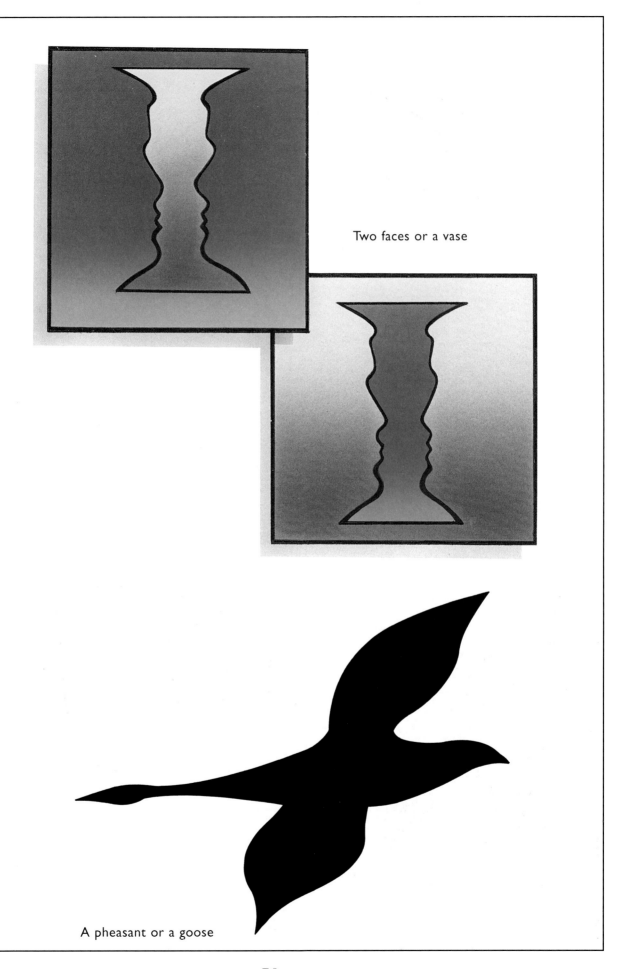

Two faces or a vase

A pheasant or a goose

An old woman or a young girl

A duck or a rabbit

An Inuit or a Native American Chief

A squirrel or a swan

A seal or a donkey

Topsy turvy
These double images reveal themselves if you look at them from a new angle. Turn the page on its side or upside-down to get a fresh perspective.

A pig or a person

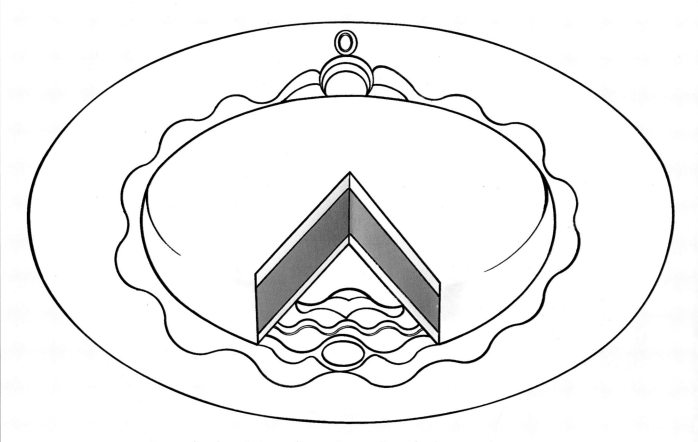

A cake missing a slice or just a slice of cake on a plate

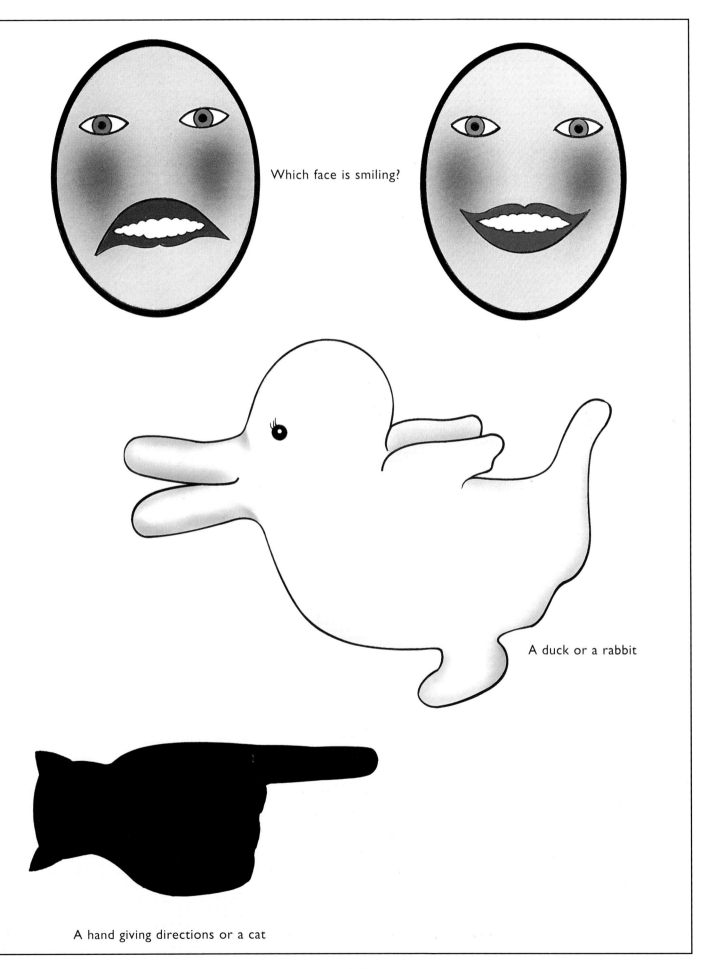

Which face is smiling?

A duck or a rabbit

A hand giving directions or a cat

POPPING PICTURES

Watch these figures turn inside out. At one moment you are looking at a tunnel and the next at a mountain. This is called perceptual reversal, when your brain keeps changing its mind about which part of the image is nearest to you and which is farthest away from you.

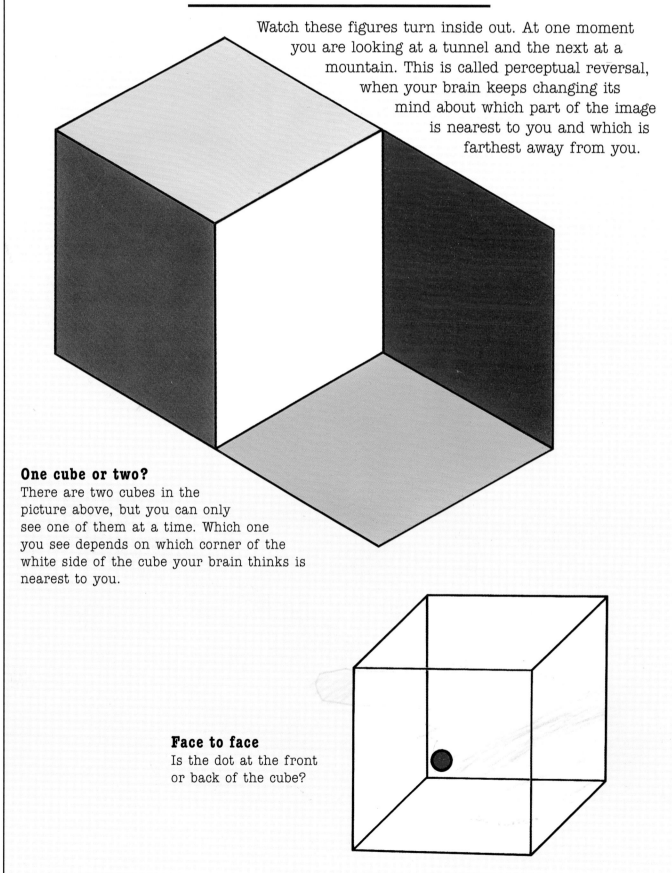

One cube or two?

There are two cubes in the picture above, but you can only see one of them at a time. Which one you see depends on which corner of the white side of the cube your brain thinks is nearest to you.

Face to face

Is the dot at the front or back of the cube?

A mountain or a tunnel?
If the smallest circle seems far away, you will see a tunnel, but if it seems close up, you will see a mountain.

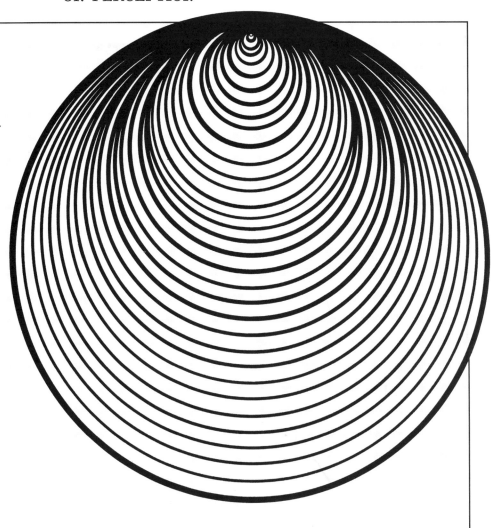

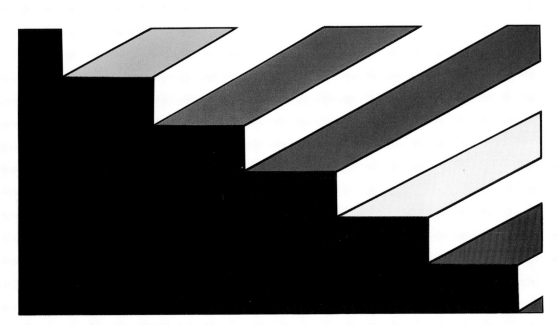

Cellar steps
Are you above the steps looking down, or are you beneath them looking up?

LOOKING FOR CLUES

Sometimes you need more information before a picture makes any sense. Look at these carefully before reading the captions. What do these images mean to you?

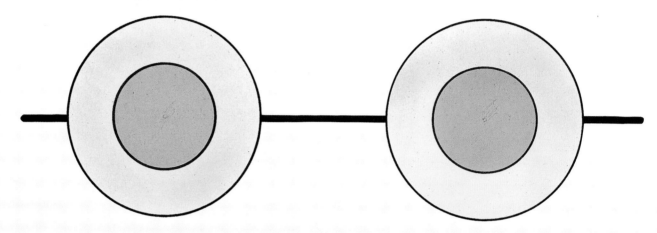

Make sense of the circles

The top picture shows two people wearing hats and riding a two-seater bicycle! Now can you see it? Can you make up other puzzles like this one?

Unfamiliar view?

Turn this page up the other way for the answer.

An inkblot world
Study this picture and you will find more than spilt ink. It is not usually this difficult to tell which shapes are the main subject of a picture and which are part of the background.

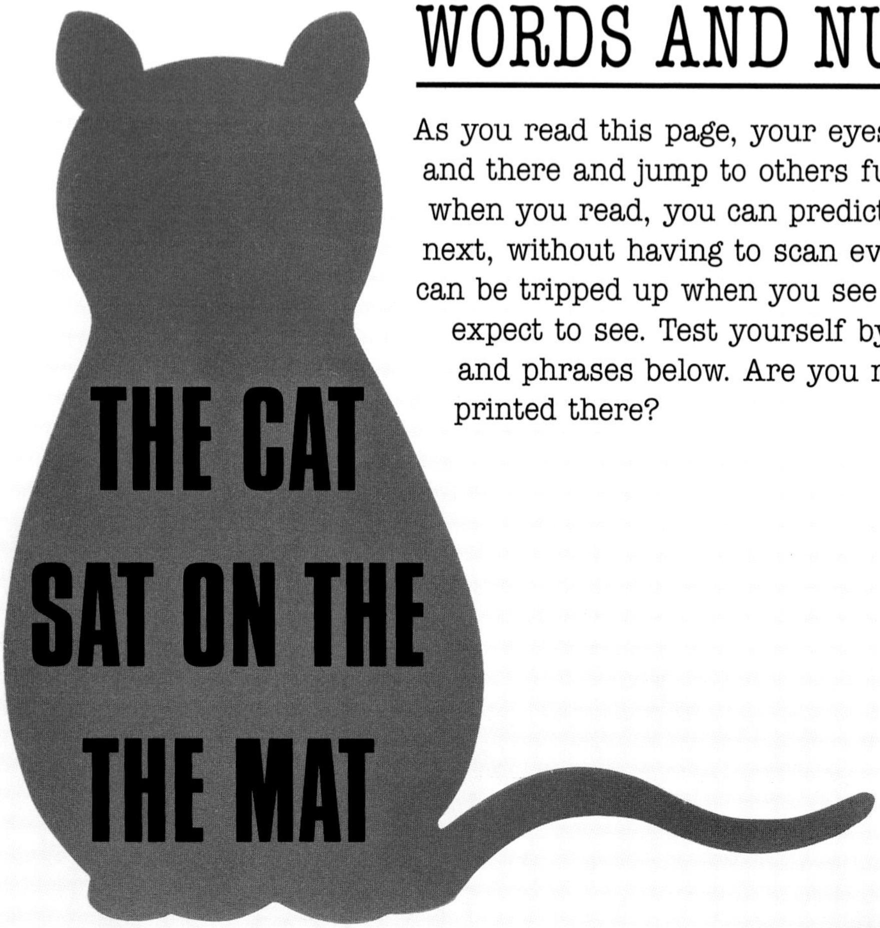

WORDS AND NUMBERS

As you read this page, your eyes skip words here and there and jump to others further along. Usually when you read, you can predict what will come next, without having to scan every word. But you can be tripped up when you see only what you expect to see. Test yourself by reading the words and phrases below. Are you really seeing what is printed there?

THE CAT
SAT ON THE
THE MAT

The added extra
What is wrong with this sentence? Can you also see the problem with the word tower on the other page?

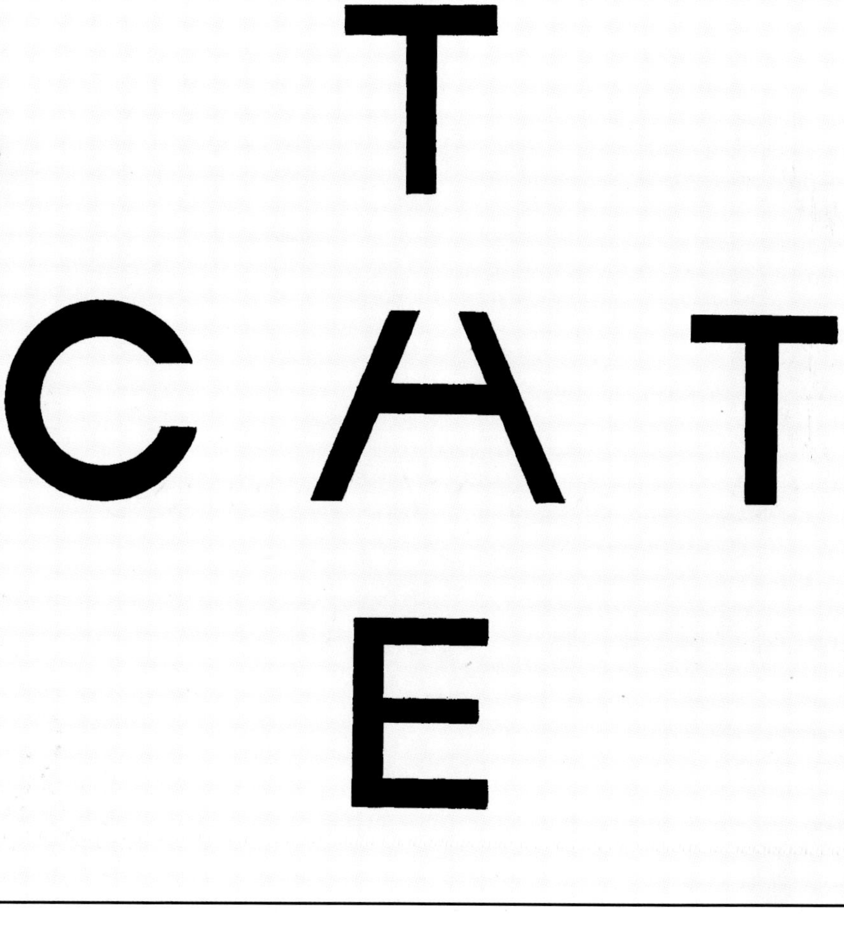

T
C A T
E

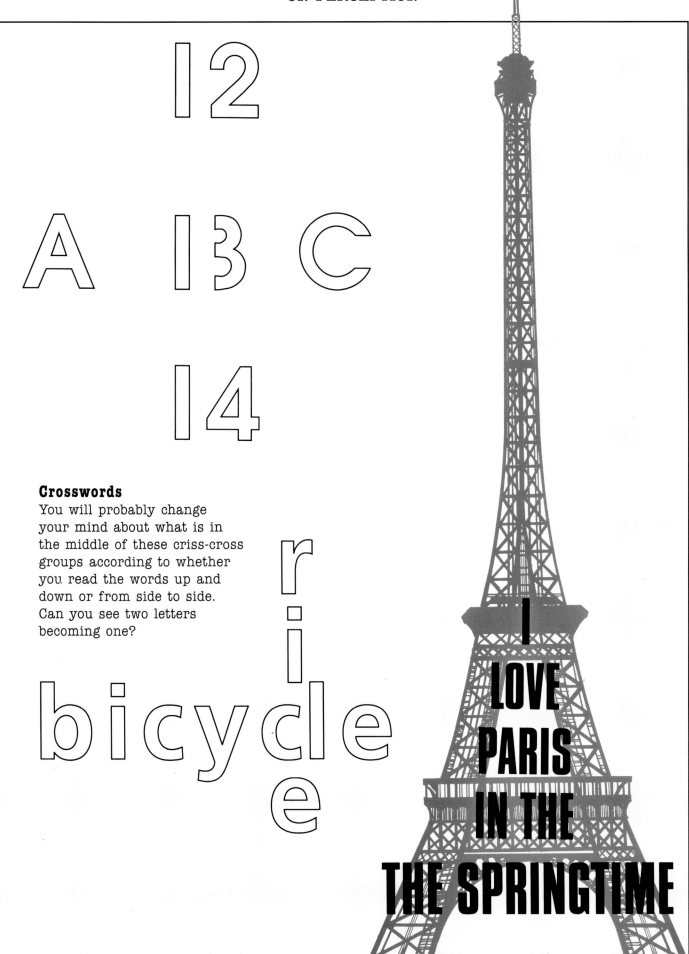

12

A 13 C

14

Crosswords
You will probably change
your mind about what is in
the middle of these criss-cross
groups according to whether
you read the words up and
down or from side to side.
Can you see two letters
becoming one?

r
i
bicycle
e

I
LOVE
PARIS
IN THE
THE SPRINGTIME

61

I spy
Can you make out all the words?
Answers at the bottom of the page.

SHADOW

Is this word really here or are you just seeing its shadow?

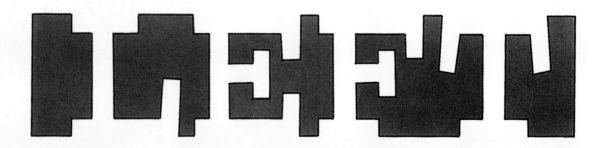

3
ON MOVEMENT

Notions that put pictures in motion

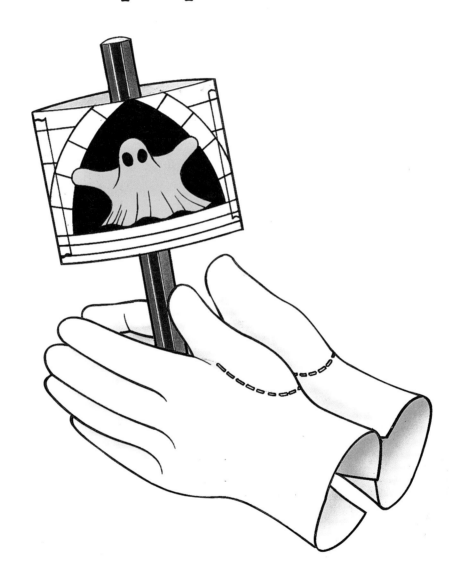

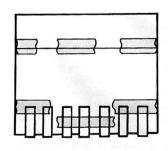

LASTING IMPRESSIONS

We take for granted the images of people, animals, cars and aircraft that roll across a screen in front of us every time we watch television, go to the movies or put on a video. They are optical illusions that are part of our everyday life. But their development depended on the invention of simple toys like these.

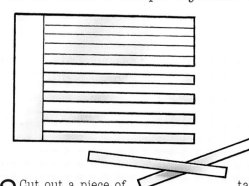

MAKE A SLIDER

This swimming whale takes a little time to prepare, but you will find it is well worth it.

1 Trace or copy the lined sheet on the other page onto a piece of white paper the same size. With some scissors, cut along each solid line right up to the dotted line. This should give you 13 thin flaps of paper. Cut off every second flap of paper along the dotted line.

2 Cut out a piece of heavy white paper (4½ x 6½ inches). Place it on top of the fringed paper with its long edge lined up against the dotted line. Fold the solid end over and tape it to the back of the paper. Fold the loose strips over and tape them down as well. Try to keep them the same distance apart. You will find it easier to tape just two or three at a time.

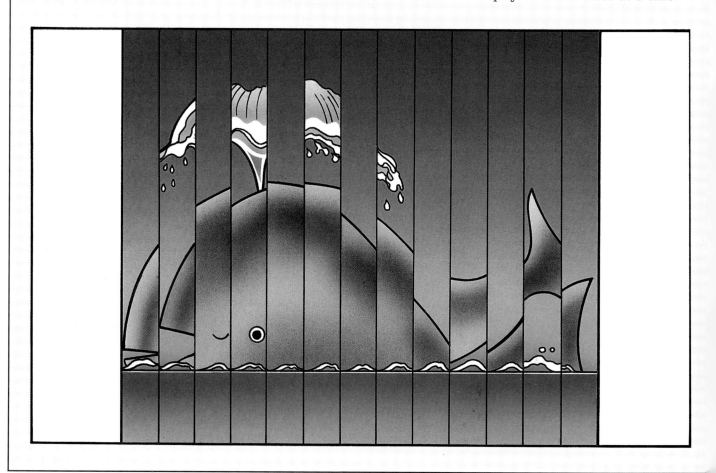

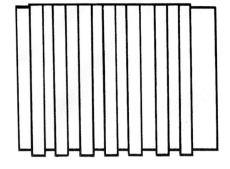

3 Carefully trace and copy onto another sheet of paper (4¼ x 11 inches) the whale (below left). Then slip this sheet into the frame so that it slides on top of the card and under the strips. Line it up with the slots of the frame so you can see the whale.

4 Now slide the strip of paper to and fro in its frame and your whale will begin to blow its top.

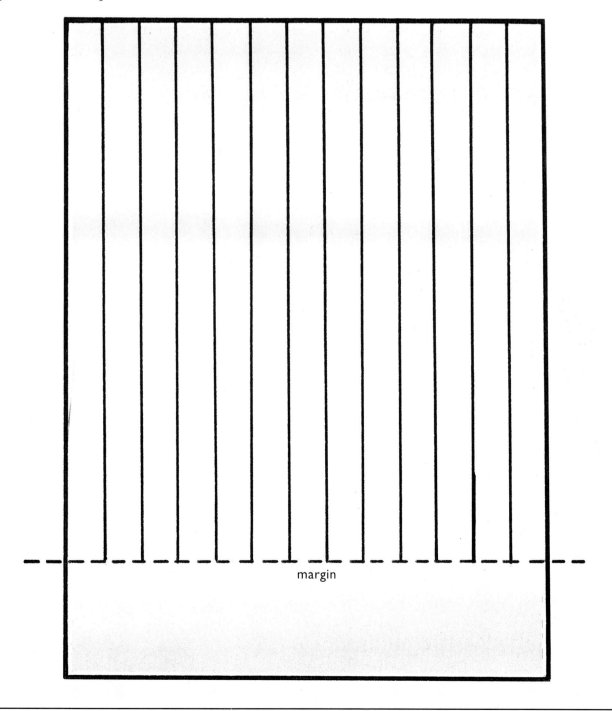

margin

MAKE A MOVIE

1 Cut a strip of white paper (1½ x 4 inches) and fold it in half.

2 Trace the left-hand image onto the middle of the first page of the paper, and the right-hand image onto the second page. You can use the pressure marks from the first drawing to line up the second one. Pencil over the two pictures so that they stand out boldly.

3 Hold the folded edge in one hand and roll the top half of the strip containing the first picture tightly around a pencil. Still holding the folded edge of the strip, rapidly move the pencil back and forth across the other half of the strip.

MAKE A FLICK BOOK

Follow the instructions below to make a permanent and professional-looking flick book, or make a simpler version with pictures of your own choice. Start with something simple like a bouncing ball, or stick people, and try to make them line up with each other. Remember that the closer one drawing is to the next, the smoother the action. The more pages the better.

1 Cut out 32 rectangles of heavy paper, all the same size as the rectangles in the strip opposite.

2 Trace each of the pictures separately onto the pages of your book. Put the pictures in number order, face up, starting with picture number 1 on the bottom. Finish with picture 32 at the top.

3 Clasp the pictures together firmly with a heavy-duty bulldog clip.

4 Hold the book in one hand by the bound edge. Flick the pages from back to front with your other hand.

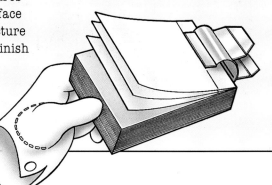

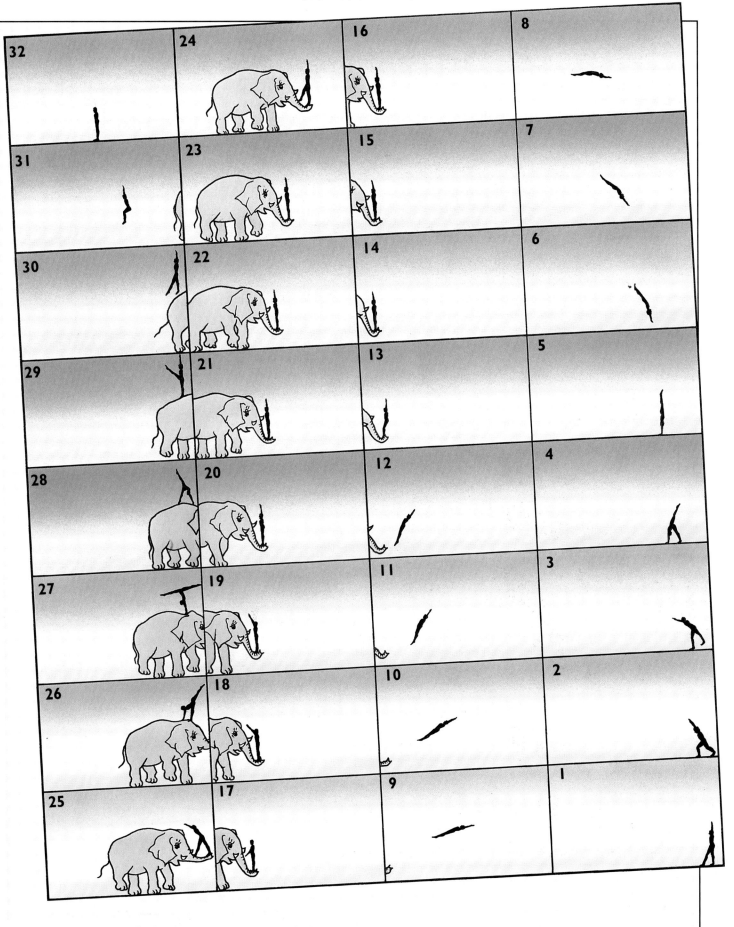

THAUMATROPES

A thaumatrope is a spinning piece of card with a picture on each side. It was invented in 1826, and was one of the earliest toys to take advantage of our brain's ability to hang on to one image and join it seamlessly to a second one. There are a number of different ways to create this simple, but effective, illusion.

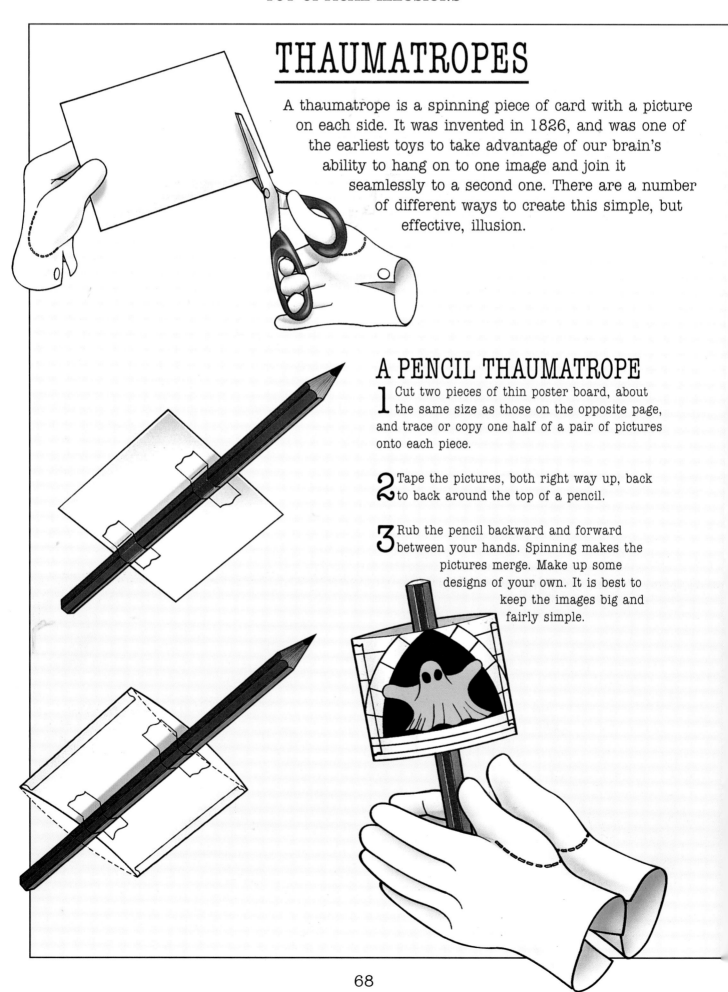

A PENCIL THAUMATROPE

1 Cut two pieces of thin poster board, about the same size as those on the opposite page, and trace or copy one half of a pair of pictures onto each piece.

2 Tape the pictures, both right way up, back to back around the top of a pencil.

3 Rub the pencil backward and forward between your hands. Spinning makes the pictures merge. Make up some designs of your own. It is best to keep the images big and fairly simple.

FREE-WHEELER

Make a free-wheeling thaumatrope in a stand.

1 Follow the instructions for the pencil thaumatrope, but stick your pictures together so that one is upside down and so that the pencil goes from side to side and not from top to bottom.

2 Cut off the top of a cereal box to leave you with a shape that fits the thaumatrope. Cut away one short side.

3 Make a hole in each side of the box big enough to fit the pencil. Gently bend back the cardboard sides to allow you to slip the thaumatrope into position. Twirl the pencil quickly to see the pictures combine.

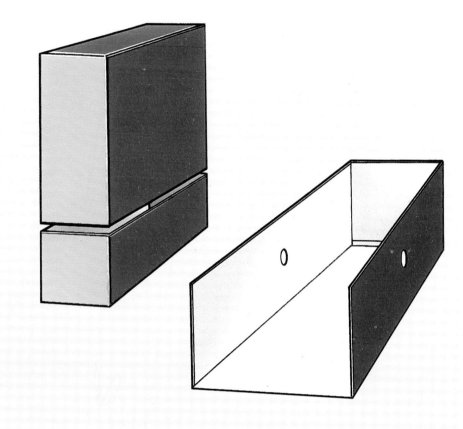

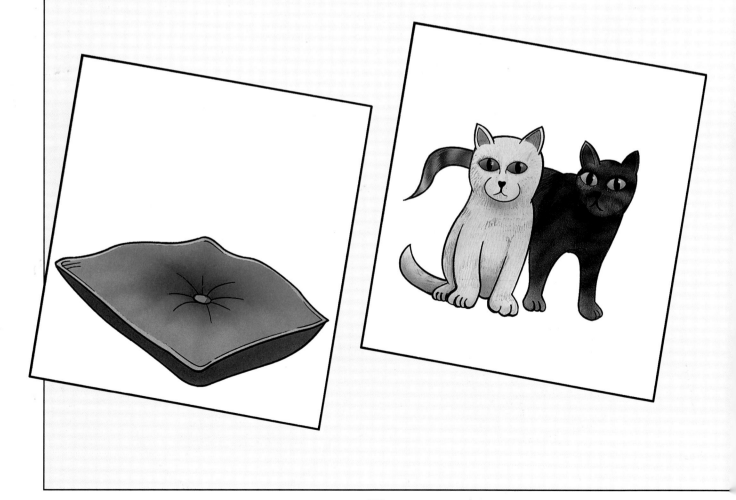

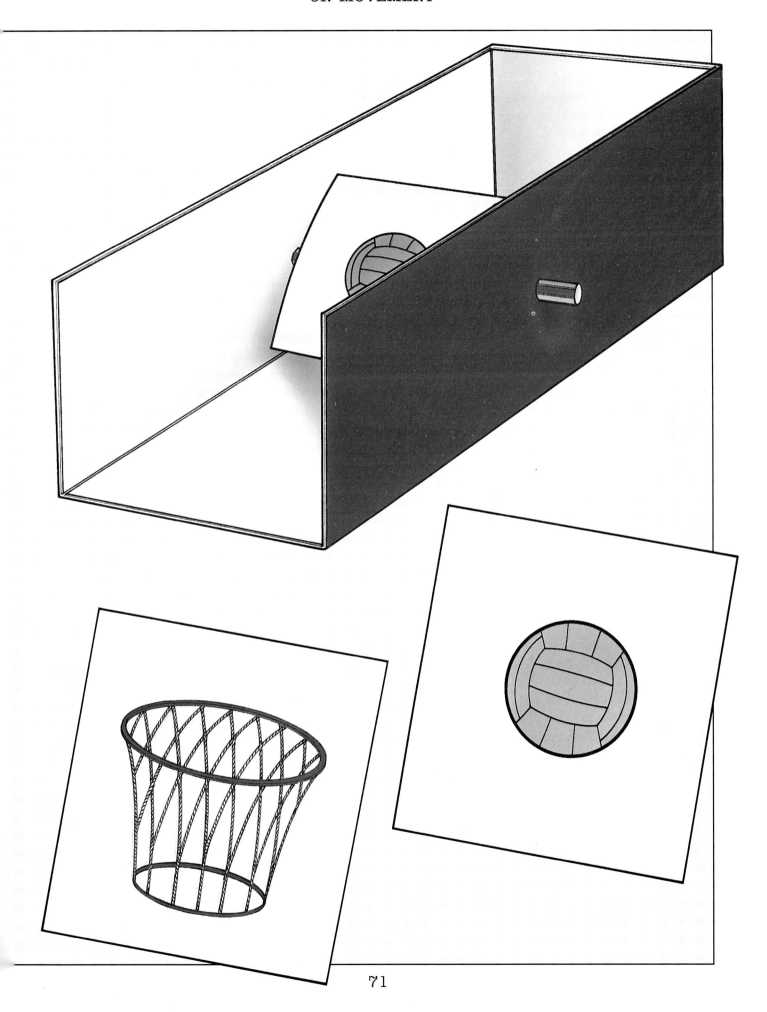

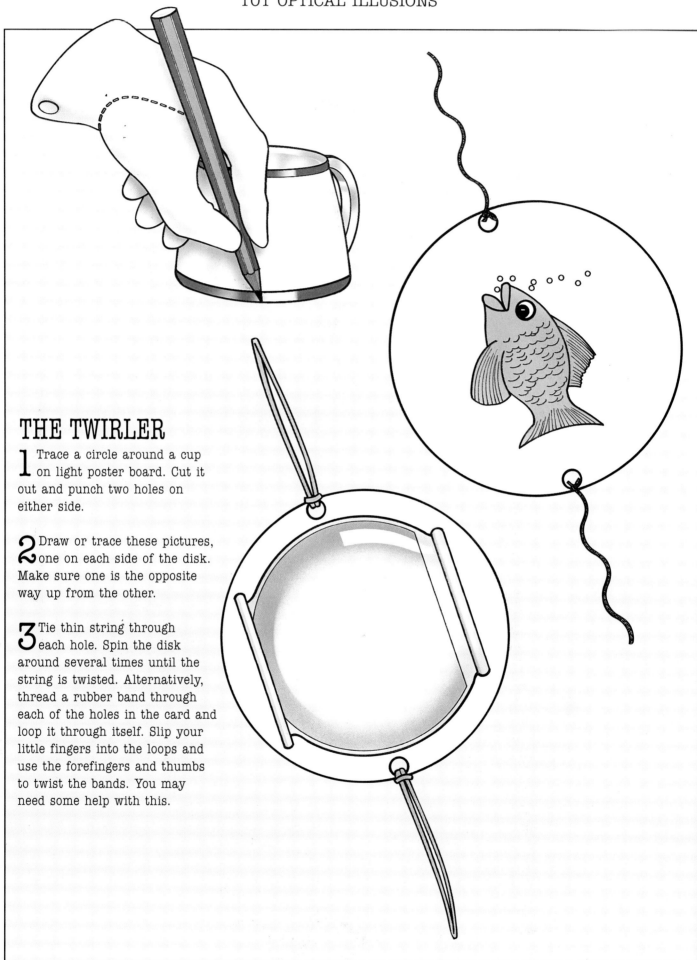

THE TWIRLER

1 Trace a circle around a cup on light poster board. Cut it out and punch two holes on either side.

2 Draw or trace these pictures, one on each side of the disk. Make sure one is the opposite way up from the other.

3 Tie thin string through each hole. Spin the disk around several times until the string is twisted. Alternatively, thread a rubber band through each of the holes in the card and loop it through itself. Slip your little fingers into the loops and use the forefingers and thumbs to twist the bands. You may need some help with this.

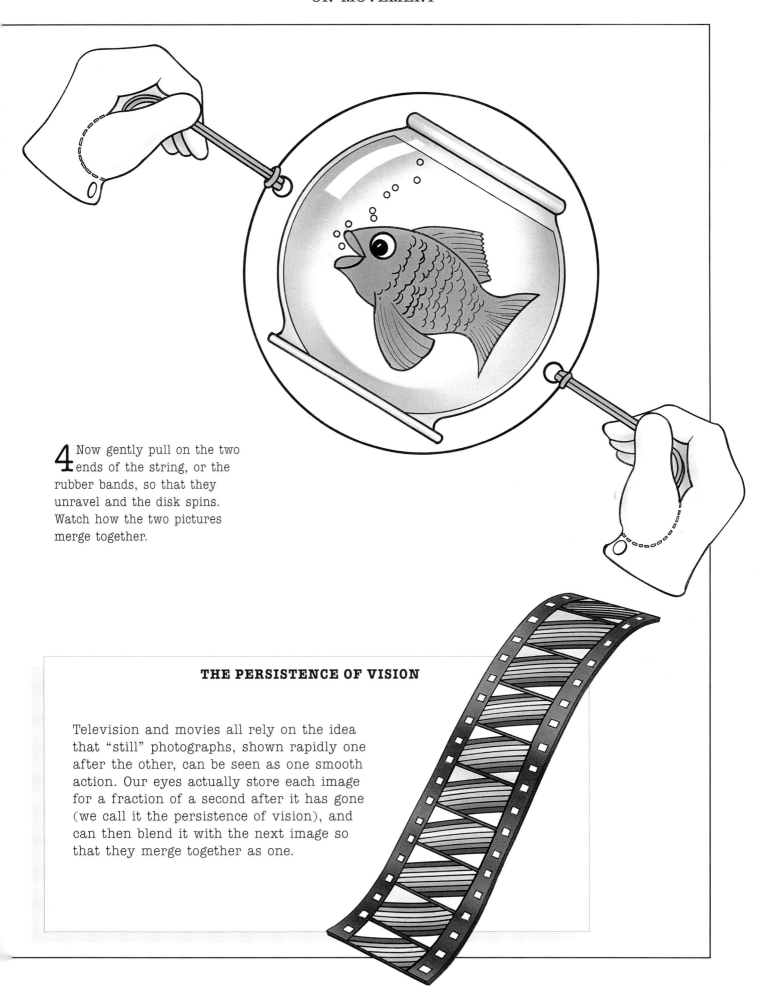

4 Now gently pull on the two ends of the string, or the rubber bands, so that they unravel and the disk spins. Watch how the two pictures merge together.

THE PERSISTENCE OF VISION

Television and movies all rely on the idea that "still" photographs, shown rapidly one after the other, can be seen as one smooth action. Our eyes actually store each image for a fraction of a second after it has gone (we call it the persistence of vision), and can then blend it with the next image so that they merge together as one.

STROBOSCOPES

A stroboscope will slow things down before your eyes. You will find that turning the slits in this stroboscope lets you see an image for only a fraction of a second at a time. You then miss a small section of the action sequence and rejoin the image a little further along, so that people running, for instance, seem to jerk along in slow motion. Anything which has a very steady and regular movement, like a wheel, looks as if it is staying quite still, while someone running appears to be in slow motion.

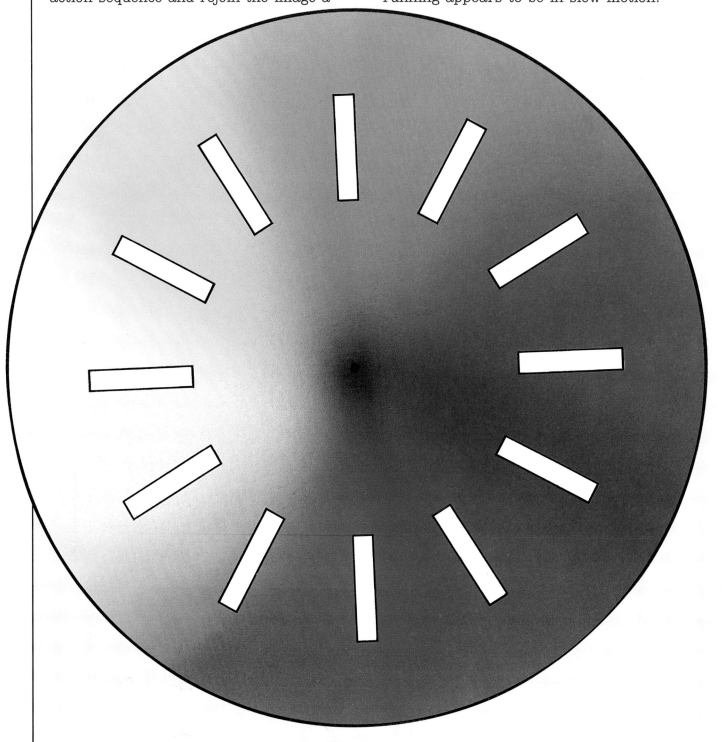

MAKE A STROBE

1 On a piece of stiff white poster board (8 inches square) trace a copy of this disk and all the slots marked on it. Cut out the disk, and then ask an adult to help you cut out the slots with an art knife.

2 Carefully paint one side of the disk black. Leave it to dry.

3 Glue an empty thread spool to the center of the black side. Let the glue dry.

4 Have a thin stick ready (a plant support or wooden skewer will do) or a pencil that will fit into the spool. Rub some soap on the end of the stick and push it into the spool. It must come all the way through, and move easily.

5 Push a pin or thumbtack, preferably with a small bead threaded onto it, through the front of the disk so that it goes into the top of the stick. Check that the disk spins easily.

6 Hold the stick in one hand so that the black side of the disk is about 10 inches in front of your eyes. Spin the disk and look through it at a moving object.

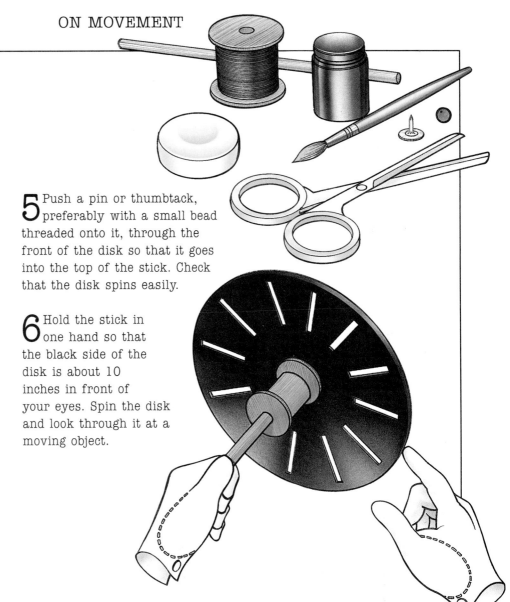

SLOW-MOTION TELEVISION

You can separate moving pictures into individual images in a rather surprising way. With the room lights on, move a pencil quickly up and down in front of a blank television screen. All that you will see of the pencil is a blur. Turn the television on, turn the lights off, and quickly swing the pencil up and down four or five times in front of the screen. The pencil looks as if it is in slow motion. The reason for this is that television pictures are sent one by one, although very quickly. Between each picture, the screen is black for a fraction of a second, and the pencil is not visible. By the time another picture is sent, the pencil has moved to a new place and you see it in separate images. You have created a simple stroboscope. It is not a good idea to watch television in a darkened room for more than a few seconds as it harms your eyes.

PHENAKISTOSCOPES

In 1834, Belgian-born Joseph Antoine Plateau discovered that if he viewed a sequence of drawings through a slit in a revolving wheel, he could create a very complex illusion of movement. His invention was known as the phenakistoscope. Later Plateau realized that his machine could also be used to make something that was already moving appear to slow down—the first stroboscope.

DANCING DOTS

Make a simple phenakistoscope which can give some great results.

1 Trace around a bowl (about 7 inches across) on stiff paper, and cut it out. Do the same with a smaller bowl (5½ inches across), using thin paper this time.

2 Make a series of evenly spaced holes with a hole punch along the edge of the large circle, 1½ inches apart and ³⁄₈ inch from the edge. (Use a piece of string marked off at every ½ inch to measure this

distance around the edge of the disk. You can use a ball point pen to punch holes, if necessary, but trim the edges of the circles to neaten them.

3 Find the center of each disk, put them together and stick them with one or two small pieces of tape.

4 On the inner disk make a series of well-formed dots with a felt-tip. Each dot should

be about the same size as the holes on the outer disk. Each dot should line up with one hole in the outer ring, but they should be a different distance away from it.

5 Stick a pin through the middle of both disks and push it into the eraser at the end of a pencil. If you prefer, you can use a tightly rolled piece of paper which you have fastened with some tape.

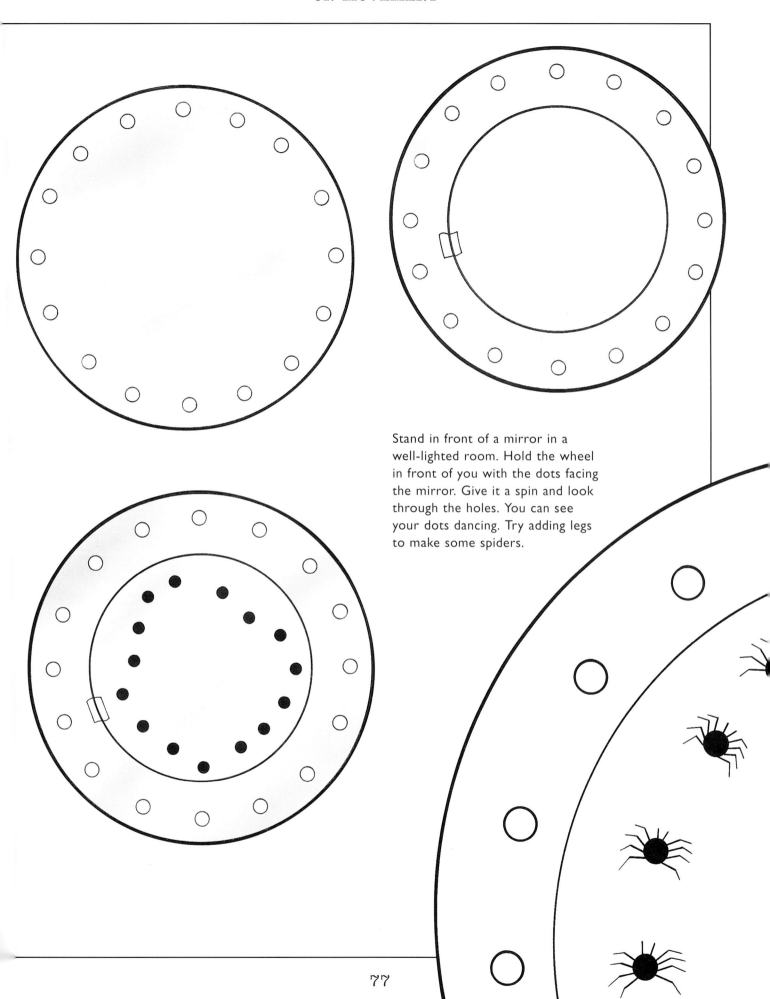

Stand in front of a mirror in a
well-lighted room. Hold the wheel
in front of you with the dots facing
the mirror. Give it a spin and look
through the holes. You can see
your dots dancing. Try adding legs
to make some spiders.

MODEL PHENAKISTOSCOPE

1 Trace one of the disks shown below onto plain stiff poster board. Then color it in carefully.

2 Cut it out and then use an art knife to cut out the rectangular slots (ask an adult to help you).

3 Push a long pin or long thin nail through a bead and then through the center of the disk. Put another bead on the pin or nail and then push it into a cork.

4 Work in a brightly lighted room. Hold the disk up to a mirror. Spin the disk clockwise by gently flicking the edge with your finger. Look through the slits and you will be able to watch the pictures move.

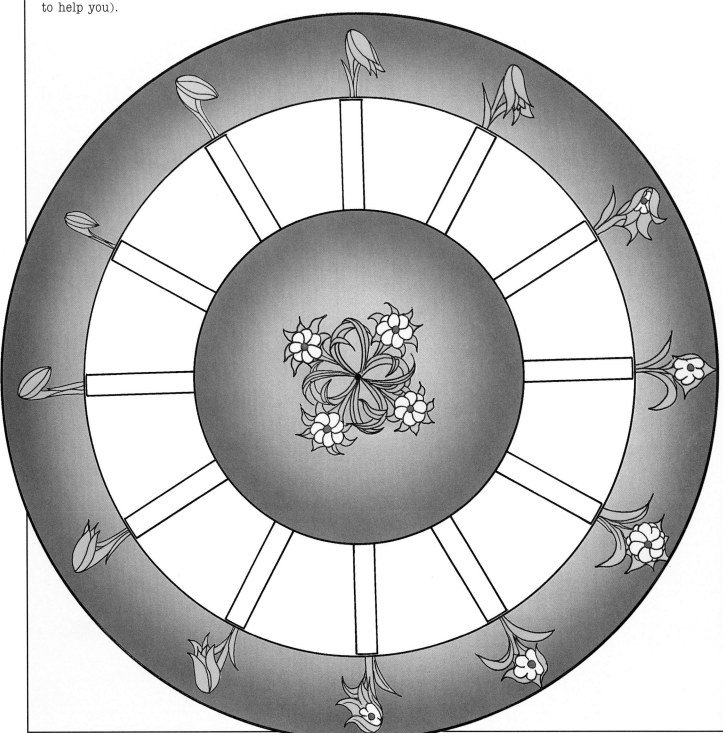

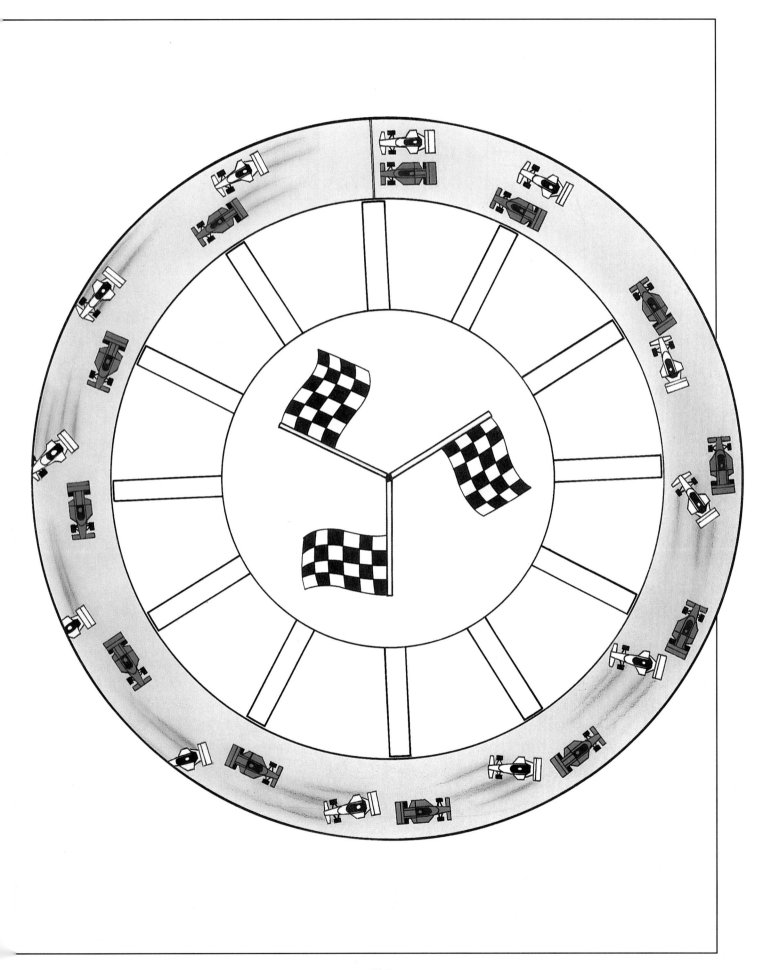

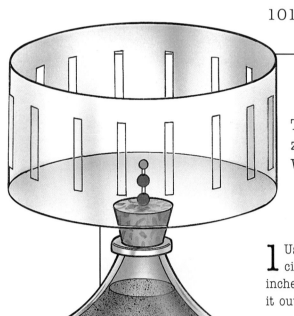

ZOETROPES

The phenakistoscope inspired other toys including the zoetrope, which an English mathematician, named William Horner, invented in about 1869.

MAKE A ZOETROPE

1 Use compasses to draw a circle with a diameter of 7 inches on thick poster board. Cut it out. Mark the center for later.

2 Cut a strip of stiff black paper (6¼ x 22¼ inches). Use a tracing of the outline on the opposite page to help you draw slits and tabs along its length. First line up the tracing with your strip and transfer the first set of outlines; then carefully move the tracing along and repeat this until the transfer is complete. Make sure all the spacing is even.

3 Cut out the tabs. Ask an adult to help you cut out the slits with an art knife.

4 Run the tip of dull scissors along the line A-B. Bend the tabs inward and glue them to the disk. Join the overlap with tape.

5 Push a bead onto a long pin or long thin nail. Push the pin or nail through the center of the zoetrope, then through another bead and then into a cork. Push the cork into a plastic bottle filled with sand or soil.

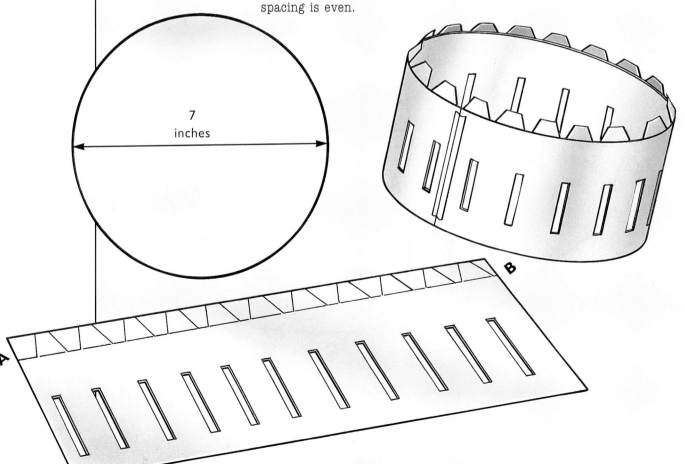

7 inches

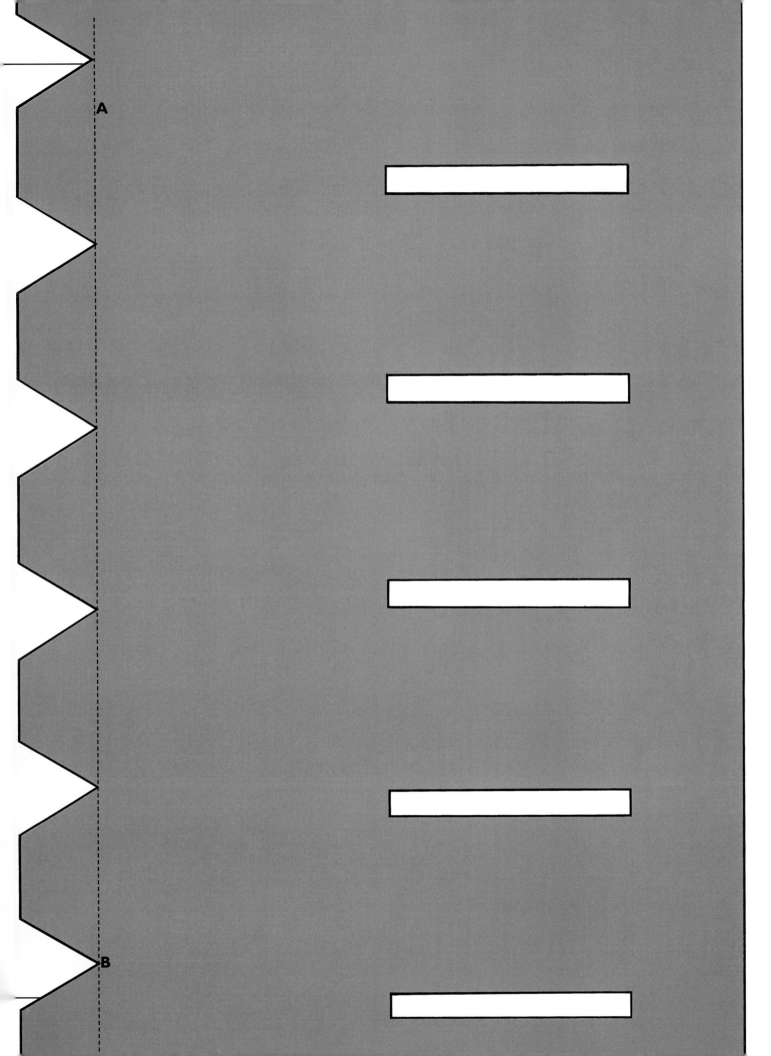

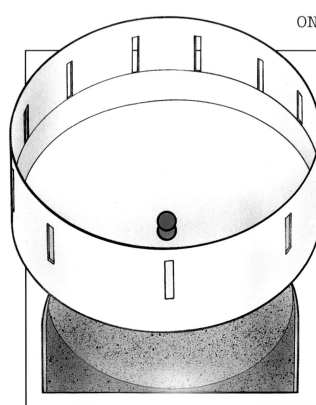

6 Trace or copy the pictures below onto a long strip of white paper. Join A to B, C to D and close the two ends to make a ring. Place your strip in the zoetrope so that it sits in the drum just below the slits.

7 Spin the zoetrope counterclockwise as you look through the slits. Can you see the figures moving? Sit back a little way from the zoetrope to get a better picture.

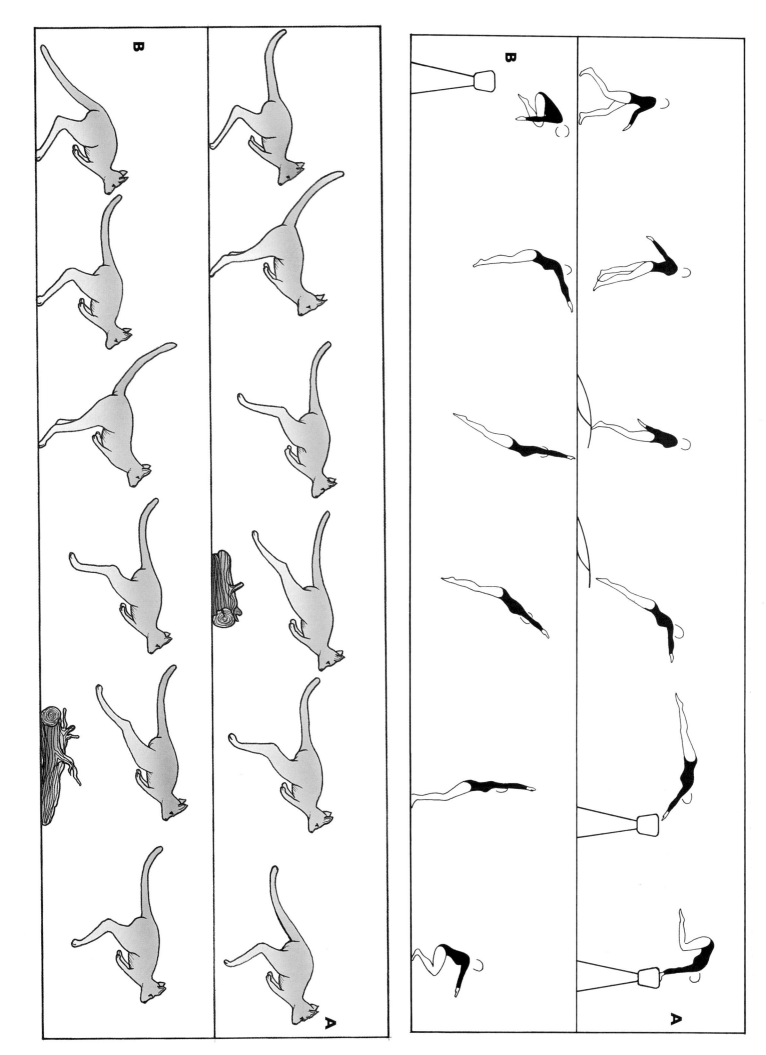

GLOSSARY

Afterimage
An image left on the retina of the eye for a short time after the object that caused it has moved away. Afterimages are formed because the cells of the retina become tired.

Anamorphic images
Specially constructed pictures where features have been distorted by "pulling" them so that they are stretched in one direction or another.

Binocular vision
Seeing a single image which has three dimensions when looking at an object with both eyes. Also called stereoscopic vision.

Blind spot
A small area at the back of the eye where there are no nerve cells sensitive to light. It is where the optic nerve leaves the eye.

Cell
A very small part of living matter.

Color
Any of the different effects of light you see in the appearance of things. Humans and some other animals are able to sense colors because of special cells, called cones, in the retina of the eye.

Color blindness
Being unable to tell the difference between some colors, usually red and green. It is due to a fault in the retina of the eye.

Concave lens
A lens which spreads out light rays passing through it. Concave lenses make objects viewed through them appear smaller.

Cone
One of the special cells in the retina of the eye which is sensitive to colours.

Convex lens
A lens which brings light rays to focus at a point. Convex lenses make objects viewed through them appear larger.

Cornea
The transparent covering at the front of the eye. The cornea covers and protects the iris and lens.

Distortion
The bending or twisting of something out of its usual shape.

Focus
The point at which light rays meet to form a clear, sharp image after passing through a lens.

Greyscale
An image made up entirely of black, white and gray tones or dots, which is created by a computer. The greyscale is used in the creation of stereograms, and forms the 3-D scene that is hidden.

Image
The picture or appearance formed by light passing through lenses, as in the eye or a camera.

Illusion
A deception or false belief.

Iris
The colorful part of the eye between the cornea and the lens. The iris controls the amount of light entering the eye.

Lens
A piece of glass, or some other transparent material, that has been given a concave or convex shape. Also, the part of the eye which focuses light onto the retina.

Light
A form of radiation that makes it possible for animals with eyes to see objects. Natural light comes from the sun, giving daylight.

Mirage
A reflected image, usually seen in the desert or along roads on hot dry days. It is created by light rays being bent, or refracted, through layers of air of different densities.

Nerve
One of the bundles of special fibres which carry impulses (messages) between the brain and spinal cord, and all the other parts of the body.

Noisefield
Used to form stereograms. A computer-generated pattern made up of one image repeated again and again. It forms the topmost surface of the stereogram and is distorted by the underlying greyscale.

Optical illusion
When the eye deceives the mind and makes a person believe something that is false.

Optic nerve
The nerve that carries impulses (messages) from the light-sensitive retina at the back of the eye to the brain.

Perception
The way we see something and understand it.

Prism
A triangular-shaped piece of glass or transparent plastic that is used to bend rays of light and to split white light into the colors of the spectrum.

Rainbow
An arc in the sky containing the colors of the spectrum. Rainbows are formed when the sun shines brightly on raindrops. The latter act as tiny prisms, breaking up the sunlight into the various colors.

Reflection
What happens when a beam of light is turned back by a surface.

Refraction
The way in which a ray of light is bent when it passes at an angle from one transparent material to another, e.g. from air into glass or water.

Retina
The light-sensitive layer of cells at the back of the eye.

Rod
One of the light-sensitive cells found in the retina of the eye. Rods are used for seeing in dim light.

Sense
One of the powers that animals possess that makes them aware of their surroundings. Humans have five main senses: sight, hearing, taste, smell and touch.

Sensitive
Able to react to a stimulus. Our eyes are sensitive to light, while our skin is sensitive to heat and touch.

Spectrum
The rainbow-colored bands of light seen when white light is split up by water droplets or a prism.

Stereoscopic vision
See Binocular vision.

Stroboscope
An instrument for determining the speed at which objects, such as wheels, rotate; a special lamp made to flash intermittently to make moving objects appear stationary.

Tear
One of the drops of salty, antiseptic liquid produced by the tear glands in the eyes. Tears keep the eyes moist and wash away dust and dirt.

Transparent
Describes any solid material or liquid that lets light pass through it and forms a clear image on the other side. Clear glass and water are transparent materials.

Vision
The ability to see; the power or sense of sight.

INDEX